D0287118

PENGUIN BOOKS

THE JOB

William S. Burroughs is the author of *Junky, Naked Lunch, The Place of Dead Roads, Cities of the Red Night, Queer, The Western Lands,* and *Interzone,* a collection of writings from the *Naked Lunch* period. He is a member of the American Academy of Arts and Letters, and a Commandeur de l'Ordre des Arts et Lettres of France. He divides his time between New York City and Lawrence, Kansas.

The Job

interviews with

William S. Burroughs

by Daniel Odier

PENGUIN BOOKS

PENGUIN BOOKS
Published by the Penguin Group
Viking Penguin Inc., 40 West 23rd Street,
New York, New York 10010, U.S.A.
Penguin Books Ltd, 27 Wrights Lane, London W8 5TZ, England
Penguin Books Australia Ltd, Ringwood, Victoria, Australia
Penguin Books Canada Ltd, 2801 John Street,
Markham, Ontario, Canada L3R 1B4
Penguin Books (N.Z.) Ltd, 182–190 Wairau Road,
Auckland 10, New Zealand

Penguin Books Ltd, Registered Offices:
Harmondsworth, Middlesex, England

First published in the United States of America by
Grove Press, Inc. 1974
Published in Penguin Books 1989

10 9 8 7 6 5 4 3 2 1

An earlier edition of this book appeared in a French translation as
Entretiens avec William Burroughs, copyright © 1969, by William
Burroughs, Daniel Odier, and Editions Pierre Belfond, Paris, France.
Portions of this book were originally published in *Books and Bookmen*
and *Mayfair*.

"Playback From Eden to Watergate" first appeared in *Harper's*
copyright © 1973 by William S. Burroughs.

"Electronic Revolution 1970–71" was originally published in a limited
edition by Blackmoor Head Press, Cambridge, copyright © 1971 by
William S. Burroughs.

LIBRARY OF CONGRESS CATALOGING IN PUBLICATION DATA
Burroughs, William S., 1914–
The job: interviews with William S. Burroughs/by Daniel Odier.
—Rev. and enl. ed.
p.   cm.
Reprint. Originally published: New York: Grove Press:
Distributed by Random House, 1974.
"Including 'Playback from Eden to Watergate' and 'Electronic
revolution 1970-71.' "
ISBN 0 14 01.1882 9 (pbk.)
1. Burroughs, William S., 1914–   —Interviews.   2. Novelists,
American—20th century—Interviews.   I. Odier, Daniel, 1945–
II. Title.
[PS3552.U75Z467   1989]   813'.54—dc19   88–22591

Printed in the United States of America
Set in Primer

From the diary of a six year old boy at the American School in Tangier Morocco: "I get up at 8:30. I eat my breakfast. Then I go to the job."

When asked what he meant by the job he said, "school of course."

The Job

Playback From
Eden to Watergate

In *Encounter Magazine*, admittedly once subsidized by the CIA, there was an article called "Night Words" by George Steiner. Talking about my writing and the writing of other writers in whose works sex scenes are frankly and explicitly described, he says, "In the name of human privacy, enough!"

In whose name is human privacy being evoked? In the name of those who bugged Martin Luther King's bedroom and ransacked the office of Ellsberg's psychiatrist? And how many other bedrooms have they bugged? Does anyone believe that these are isolated instances? That they were caught on the first job? Who is casting the first stone here?

It is precisely by breaking down the whole concept of privacy that the monopoly the Nixon Administration wishes to set up will be broken down. When nobody cares, then shame ceases to exist and we can all return to the Garden of Eden without any God prowling around like a house dick with a tape recorder. Books and films in which the sex act is explicitly represented are certainly a step in the right direction. It is precisely this breakdown of shame and fear with regard to sex that the Nixon Administration is all out to stop so it can continue to use shame and fear as weapons of political control.

It is generally assumed that the spoken word came before the written word. I suggest that the spoken word as we know it came after the written word. In the beginning was the Word, and the Word was God—and the word was flesh . . . human flesh . . . in the beginning of *writing*. Animals talk. They don't write. Now, a wise old rat may know a lot about traps and poison but he cannot write "Death Traps in Your Warehouse" for the *Reader's Digest*, with tactics for ganging up on dogs and ferrets and taking care of wise guys who stuff steel wool up ratholes. It is doubtful that the spoken word would ever have evolved beyond the animal stage without the written word. The written word is inferential in human speech.

My basic theory is that the written word was actually a virus that made the spoken word possible. The word has not been recognized as a virus because it has achieved a state of stable symbiosis with the host, though this symbiotic relationship is now breaking down, for reasons I will suggest later.

I quote from *Mechanisms of Virus Infection*, edited by Mr. Wilson Smith, a scientist who really thinks about his subject instead of merely correlating data. What he thinks about is the ultimate intention of the virus organism. In a chapter entitled "Virus Adaptability and Host Resistance," by G. Belyavin, speculations as to the biologic goal of the virus species are enlarged. "Viruses are obligatory cellular parasites and are thus wholly dependent upon the integrity of the cellular systems they parasitize for their survival in an active state. It is something of a paradox that many viruses ultimately destroy the cells in which they are living."

Is the virus then simply a time bomb left on this planet to be activated by remote control? An extermination program in fact? In its path from full virulence to its ultimate goal of symbiosis, will any human creature survive?

"Taking the virus-eye view, the ideal situation would appear to be one in which the virus replicates in cells without in any way disturbing their normal metabolism. This has been suggested as the ideal biological situation toward which all viruses are slowly evolving."

Would you offer violence to a well-intentioned virus on its slow road to symbiosis?

"It is worth noting that if a virus were to attain a state of wholly benign equilibrium with its host cell it is unlikely that its presence would be readily detected or that it would necessarily be recognized as a virus." I suggest that the word is just such a virus. Dr. Kurt Unruh von Steinplatz has put forward an interesting theory as to the origins and history of this word virus. He postulates that the word was a virus of what he calls *"biologic mutation"* affecting a change in its host which was then genetically conveyed. One reason that apes can't talk is because the structure of their inner throats is simply not designed to formulate words. He postulates that alterations in inner throat structure were occasioned by a virus illness. And vot an occasion! This illness may well have had a high rate of mortality, but some female apes must have survived to give birth to the *Wunderkinder*. The illness perhaps assumed a more malignant form in the male because of his more developed and rigid muscular structure, causing death through strangulation and vertebral fracture. Since the virus in both male and female precipitates sexual fenzy through irritation of sex centers in the brain, the male impregnated the females in their death spasms and the altered throat structure was genetically conveyed. *Ach, Junge,* what a scene is here . . . the apes are molting fur, steaming off, the females whimpering and slobbering over the dying males like cows with aftosa, and so a stink—musky, sweet, rotten-metal stink of the forbidden fruit in the Garden of Eden. . . .

The creation of Adam, the Garden of Eden, Adam's fainting spell during which God made Eve from his body, the forbidden fruit, which was of course knowledge of the whole stinking thing and might be termed the first Watergate scandal, all slots neatly into Doc von Steinplatz's theory. And this was a *white* myth. This leads us to the supposition that the word virus assumed a specially malignant and lethal form in the white race. What then accounts for this special malignance of the white word virus? Most likely a virus mutation occasioned by radioactivity. All animal and insect experiments so far carried out indicate that mutations resulting from radiation are unfavorable—that is, not conducive to survival. These experiments relate to the effect of radiation on autonomous creatures. What about the effects of radiation on viruses? Are there not perhaps some so-classified and secret experiments hiding behind national security? Virus mutations occasioned by radiation may be quite favorable for the virus. And such a virus might well violate the ancient covenant of symbiosis, the benign equilibrium with the host cell. So now, with the tape recorders of Watergate and the fallout from atomic testing, the virus stirs uneasily in all your white throats. It was a killer virus once. It could become a killer virus again and rage through cities of the world like a topping forest fire.

"It is the beginning of the end." That was the reaction of a science attaché at one of Washington's major embassies to reports that a synthetic gene particle had been produced in the laboratory. "Any small country can now make a virus for which there is no cure. It would take only a small laboratory. Any small country with good biochemists could do it."

And presumably any big country could do it quicker and better.

I advance the theory that in the electronic revolution a virus *is* a very small unit of word and image. I have suggested how such units can be biologically activated to act as communicable virus strains. Let us start with three tape recorders in the Garden of Eden. Tape recorder one is Adam. Tape recorder two is Eve. Tape recorder three is God, who deteriorated after Hiroshima into the Ugly American. Or, to return to our primeval scene: tape recorder one is the male ape in a helpless sexual fenzy as the virus strangles him. Tape recorder two is the cooing female ape who straddles him. Tape recorder three is DEATH.

Von Steinplatz postulates that the virus of biologic mutation, which he calls Virus B-23, is contained in the word. Unloosing this virus from the word could be more deadly than unloosing the power of the atom. Because all hate, all pain, all fear, all lust is contained in the word.

We now have three tape recorders. So we will make a simple word virus. Let us suppose that our target is a rival politician. On tape recorder one we will record speeches and conversations, carefully editing in stammers, mispronunciations, inept phrases—the worst number one we can assemble. Now, on tape recorder two we will make a love tape by bugging his bedroom. We can potentiate this tape by splicing it with a sexual object that is inadmissible or inaccessible or both, say, the Senator's teen-age daughter. On tape recorder three we will record hateful, disapproving voices. We'll splice the three recordings in together at very short intervals and play them back to the Senator and his constituents. This cutting and playback can be very complex, involving speech scramblers and batteries of tape recorders but *the basic principle is simply splicing sex tapes and disapproval tapes together.* Once the association lines are established, they are activated every time the Senator's speech centers are activated, which is all the time (heaven help that sorry bastard if anything happened to his big mouth). So his teen-age daughter crawls all over him while Texas Rangers and decent church-going women rise from tape recorder three screaming "WHAT ARE YOU DOING IN FRONT OF DECENT PEOPLE!"

The teen-age daughter is just a refinement. Basically all you need are sex recordings on number two and hostile recordings on number three. With this simple formula any CIA son of a bitch can become God—that is, tape recorder three. Notice the emphasis on sexual material in burglaries and bugging in the Watergate cesspool—bugging Martin Luther King's bedroom. Kiss kiss bang bang. A deadly assassination technique. At the very least sure to unnerve opponents and put them at a disadvantage. So the real scandal of Watergate that has not come out yet is not that bedrooms were bugged and the offices of psychiatrists ransacked but the precise use that was made of this sexual material.

This formula works best on a closed circuit. If sexual recordings and films are widespread, tolerated, and publicly shown, tape recorder three loses its power. Which perhaps explains why the Nixon Administration is out to close down sex films and reestablish censorship of all films and books—to keep tape recorder three on closed circuit.

And this brings us to the subject of SEX. In the words of the late John O'Hara, "I'm glad you came to me instead of one of those quacks on the top floor." Psychiatrists, priests, whatever they call themselves, they want to turn it off and keep tape recorder three in business. Let's turn it on. All you swingers use movie cameras and tape recorders to record and photograph your sessions. Now go over the session and pick out the sexiest pieces —you know, when it really happens. Reich built a machine with electrodes to be attached to the penis to measure this orgasm charge. Here is an unpleasurable orgasm sagging ominously as tape recorder three cuts in. He just made it. And here is a pleasurable orgasm way up on the graph. So take all the best of your sessions and invite the neighbors to see it. It's the neighborly thing to do. Try cutting them in together, alternating twenty-four frames per second. Try slowdowns and speedups. Build and experiment with an orgone accumulator. It's simply a box of any shape or size lined with iron. Your intrepid reporter at age thirty-seven achieved spontaneous orgasm, no hands, in an orgone accumulator built in an orange grove in Pharr, Texas. It was the small, direct-application accumulator that did the trick. That's what every red-blooded boy and girl should be doing in the basement workshop. The orgone accumulator could be greatly potentiated by using *magnetized iron*, which sends a powerful magnetic field through the body. And small accumulators like ray guns.

There is two-gun Magee going off in his pants. The gun falls from his hand. Quick as he was he was not quick enough.

For a small directional accumulator obtain six powerful magnets. Arrange your magnetized iron squares so that they form a box. In one end of the box drill a hole and insert an iron tube. Now cover the box and tube with any organic material—rubber, leather, cloth. Now train the tube on your privates and the privates of your friends and neighbors. It's good for young and old, man and beast, and is known as SEX. It is also known to have a direct connection with what is known as LIFE. Let's get St. Paul off our backs and take off the Bible Belt. And tell tape recorder three to cover his own dirty thing. It stinks from the Garden of Eden to Watergate.

I have said that the real scandal of Watergate is the use made of recordings. And what is this use? Having made the recordings as described, what then do they do with them?

Answer: *They play them back on location.*

They play these recordings back to the target himself, if the target is an individual, from passing cars and agents that walk by him in the street. They play these recordings back in his neighborhood. Finally they play them back in subways, restaurants, airports, and other public places. *Playback* is the essential ingredient.

I have made a number of experiments with street recordings and playbacks over a period of years, and the startling fact emerges that you *do not need sex recordings or even doctored tapes to produce effects by playback. Any recordings played back on location in the manner I will now describe can produce effects.* No doubt sexual and doctored tapes would be more powerful. But some of the power in the word is released by simple playback, as anyone can verify who will take the time to experiment.

I have frequently observed that this simple operation—making recordings and taking pictures of some location you wish to discommode or destroy, then playing recordings back and taking more pictures—will result in accidents, fires, removals, especially the last. The target moves. We carried out this operation with the Scientology Center at 37 Fitzroy Street. Some months later they moved to 68 Tottenham Court Road, where a similar operation was recently carried out.

Here is a sample operation carried out against the Moka Bar at 29 Frith Street, London, W.1, beginning on August 3, 1972. Reverse Thursday. Reason for operation was outrageous and unprovoked discourtesy and poisonous cheesecake. Now to close in on the Moka Bar. Record. Take pictures. Stand around outside. Let them see me. They are seething around in there. The horrible old proprietor, his frizzy-haired wife and slack-jawed son, the snarling counterman. I have them and they know it.

"You boys have a rep for making trouble. Well, come on out and make some. Pull a camera-breaking act, and I'll call a bobby. I got a right to do what I like in the public street."

If it came to that, I would explain to the policeman that I was taking street recordings and making a documentary of Soho. This was after all London's first espresso bar, was it not? I was doing them a favor. They couldn't say what both of us knew without being ridiculous.

"He's not making any documentary. He's trying to blow up the coffee machine, start a fire in the kitchen, start fights in here, get us a citation from the Board of Health."

Yes, I had them and they knew it. I looked in at the old prop. and smiled, as if he would like what I was doing. Playback would come later with more pictures. I took my time and strolled over to the Brewer Street Market, where

I recorded a three-card monte game. Now you see it, now you don't.

Playback was carried out a number of times with more pictures. Their business fell off. They kept shorter and shorter hours. October 30, 1972, the Moka Bar closed. The location was taken over by the Queen's Snack Bar.

How to apply the three-tape-recorder analogy to this simple operation. Tape recorder one is the Moka Bar itself in its pristine condition. Tape recorder two is my recording of the Moka Bar vicinity. These recordings are access. Tape recorder two in the Garden of Eden was Eve made from Adam. So a recording made from the Moka Bar is a piece of the Moka Bar. The recording once made, this piece becomes autonomous and out of their control. Tape recorder three is playback. Adam experiences shame when his disgraceful behavior is played back to him by tape recorder three, which is God.

By playing back my recordings to the Moka Bar when I want and with any changes I wish to make in recordings, I become God for this locale. I affect them. They cannot affect me.

Suppose, for example, that in the interest of national security, your bathroom and bedroom are bugged and rigged with hidden infrared cameras. These pictures and recordings give access. You may not experience shame during defecation and intercourse, but you may well experience shame when these recordings are played back to a disapproving audience. Shame is playback: exposure to disapproval.

Now let us consider the arena of politics and the applications of bugging in this area. Of course, any number of recordings are immediately available since politicians make speeches on TV. These recordings, however, do not give access. The man who is making a speech is not really there. Consequently, intimate or at least private recordings are needed, which is why the Watergate conspirators found it necessary to resort to burglary.

A Presidential candidate is not a sitting duck like the Moka Bar. He can make any number of recordings of his opponents. So the game is complex and competitive, with recordings made by both sides. This leads to more sophisticated techniques, the details of which have yet to come out.

The basic operation of recording, pictures, more pictures, and playback can be carried out by anyone with a recorder and a camera. Any number can play. Millions of people carrying out this basic operation could nullify the control system which those who are behind Watergate and Nixon are attempting to impose. Like all control systems, it depends on maintaining a monopoly position. If anybody can be tape recorder three, then tape recorder three loses power. God must be *the* God.

London, 1973   William S. Burroughs

"Navigare necesse es. Vivare no es necesse."

"It is necessary to travel. It is not necessary to live." These words inspired early navigators when the vast frontier of unknown seas opened to their sails in the fifteenth century. Space is the new frontier. Is this frontier open to youth? I quote from the *London Express*, December 30, 1968: "If you are a fit young man under twenty-five with lightning reflexes who fears nothing in heaven or on the earth and has a keen appetite for adventure don't bother to apply for the job of astronaut." They want "cool dads" trailing wires to the "better half" from an aqualung. Doctor Paine of the Space Center in Houston says: "This flight was a triumph for the squares of this world who aren't hippies and work with slide rules and aren't ashamed to say a prayer now and then." Is this the great adventure of space? Are these men going to take the step into regions literally unthinkable in verbal terms? To travel in space you must leave the old verbal garbage behind: God talk, country talk, mother talk, love talk, party talk. You must learn to exist with no religion no country no allies. You must learn to live alone in silence. Anyone who prays in space is not there.

The last frontier is being closed to youth. However there are many roads to space. To achieve complete freedom from past conditioning is to be in space. Techniques exist for achieving such freedom. These techniques are being concealed and withheld. In *The Job* I consider techniques of discovery.

Author's Foreword

This book was originally conceived as a series of impromptu interviews. However, as Monsieur Odier asked questions I found that I had in many cases already answered these questions in various books, articles and short pieces. So instead of paraphrasing or summarizing I inserted the indicated material. The result is interview form presented as a film with fade-outs and flash-back *illustrating* the answers.

one
Journey through time-space

QUESTION : Your books, since The Ticket that Exploded especially, are no longer "novels"; a breaking up of novelistic form is noticeable in Naked Lunch. Toward what end or goal is this break-up heading?

ANSWER : That's very difficult to say. I think that the novelistic form is probably outmoded and that we may look forward perhaps to a future in which people do not read at all or read only illustrated books and magazines or some abbreviated form of reading matter. To compete with television and photo magazines writers will have to develop more precise techniques producing the same effect on the reader as a lurid action photo.

Q : What separates Naked Lunch from Nova Express? What is the most important evolution between these two books?

A : I would say that the introduction of the cut-up and fold-in method which occurred between Naked Lunch and Nova Express is undoubtedly the most important evolution between these books. In Nova Express I think I get further from the conventional novel form than I did in Naked Lunch. I don't feel that Nova Express is in any sense a wholly successful book.

Q : You wrote: "Writing is fifty years behind painting." How can the gap be closed?

A : I did not write that. Mr Brion Gysin who is both painter and writer wrote "writing is fifty years behind painting." Why this gap? Because the painter can touch and handle his medium and the writer cannot. The writer does not yet know what words are. He deals only with abstractions from the source point of words. The painter's ability to touch and handle his medium led to montage techniques sixty years ago. It is to be hoped that the extension of cut-up techniques will lead to more precise verbal experiments closing this gap and giving a whole new dimension to writing. These techniques can show the writer what words are and put him in tactile communication with his medium. This in turn could lead to a precise science of words and show how certain word combinations produce certain effects on the human nervous system.

Q : Did you use the techniques of fold-up and cut-up for a long time before moving on to the use of the tape recorder? What were your most interesting experiences with the earlier technique?

A : The first extension of the cut-up method occurred through the use of tape recorders and this extension was introduced by Mr Brion Gysin. The simplest tape recorder cut-up is made by recording some material and then cutting in passages at random—of course the words are wiped off the tape where these cut-ins occur—and you get very interesting juxtapositions. Some of them are useful from a literary point of view and some are not. I would say that my most interesting experience with the earlier techniques was the realization that when you make cut-ups you do not get simply random juxtapositions of words, that they do mean something, and often that these meanings refer to some future event. I've made many cut-ups and then later recognized that the cut-up referred to something that I read later in a newspaper or in a book, or something that happened. To give a very simple example, I made a cut-up of something Mr. Getty had written, I believe for Time and Tide. The following phrase emerged: "It's a bad thing to sue your own father." About three years later his son sued him. Perhaps events are pre-written and pre-recorded and when you cut word lines the future leaks out. I have seen enough examples to convince me that the cut-ups are a basic key to the nature and function of words.

Q : For you the tape recorder is a device for breaking down the barriers which surround consciousness. How did you come to use tape recorders? What is the advantage of that technique over the fold-in cut-up technique?

A : Well, I think that was largely the influence of Mr Brion Gysin who pointed out that the cut-up method could be carried much further on tape recorders. Of course you can do all sorts of things on tape recorders which can't be done anywhere else—effects of simultaneity, echoes, speed-ups, slow-downs, playing three tracks at once, and so forth. There are all sorts of things you can do on a tape recorder that cannot possibly be indicated on a printed page. The concept of simultaneity cannot be indicated on a printed page except very crudely through the use of columns and even so the reader must follow one column down. We're used to reading from left to right and then back, and this conditioning is not easy to break down.

Q : When you have arrived at a mix or montage, do you follow the channels opened by the text or do you adapt what you want to say to the mix?

A : I would say I follow the channels opened by the re-arrangement of the text. This is the most important function of the cut-up. I may take a page, cut it up, and get a whole new idea for straight narrative, and not use any of the cut-up material at all, or I may use a sentence or two out of the actual cut-up.

It's not unconscious at all, it's a very definite operation...the simplest way is to take a page, cut it down the middle and across the middle, and then rearrange the four sections. Now that's a very simple form of cut-up if you want to get some idea of one rearrangement of the words on that page. It's quite conscious, there's nothing of automatic writing or unconscious procedure involved here.

You don't know what you're going to get simply because of the limitations of the human mind any more than the average person can plan five moves ahead in chess. Presumably it would be possible for someone with a photographic memory to look at a page and cut it up in his mind, that is, put these words up here and those up there... I've recently written a film script on the life of Dutch Schultz, now this is perfectly straight writing. Nonetheless I cut up every page and suddenly got a lot of new ideas that were then incorporated into the structure of the narrative. This is a perfectly straight film treatment, quite intelligible to the average reader, in no sense experimental writing.

Q : Does anyone anticipate using cut-up in the film?

A : Cut-ups have been used in films for a long time. In fact films are assembled in the cutting room. Like the painter film technicians can touch and handle their medium move pieces of it around and try out new juxtapositions. For example in a straight narrative passage here is a delirium scene or someone in a confused state of mind remembering past events... The writer can of course construct such a scene consciously and artistically. My method is to type out the material to be used and then strain it through several cut-up procedures. In this way I find a more realistic picture of delirium emerges than could be reached by artificial reconstruction. You are handling as it were the materials and processes of delirium. I make a number of cut-ups and select the ones finally that seem to me the most successful. The selection and arrangement of materials is quite conscious but there is a random factor by which I obtain the material which I use then, select and work over into an acceptable form.

Q : To what degree do you control what you put into your montages?

A : Well you control what you put into your montages; you don't fully control what comes out. That is, I select a page to cut up and I have control over what I put in.

I simply fit what comes out of the cut-ups back into a narrative structure.

Q : Do you work while you're traveling on trains or boats?

A : I have done this, particularly on trains, if I have a drawing room and a desk. I don't travel very often on boats. . . I have made the attempt on a train of making montages of what I saw out the window and these attempts were described in an interview in the *Paris Review*, that is one example of a train trip in which I tried typing, incorporating what I saw in the passing stations, and also taking pictures. Merely an experiment. . .

Q : When you have taken raw, real materials from life by various means, do you always project them into another space-time?

A : I do in many cases, for example you'll read something in a newspaper or see something in the street, pick up a character maybe from someone you see in the street, then you transform the character and change the setting.

Q : Do you use photographs or films along with tape recordings? Films with a matching sound track? How does the resulting juxtaposition of different materials work out?

A : I have done quite a lot of experimentation of making tape recordings and taking films at the same time and have accumulated some rather odd results and experiences all quite inconclusive, interesting, but not actually very applicable to writing . . . There're many possibilities here, many suggestions and ideas I've had for new effects in film. For example you take a television set, shut off the sound track and put on any arbitrary sound track and it will seem to fit. You show a bunch of people running for a bus in Piccadilly and put in machine-gun sound effects and it will look like Petrograd in 1917, people will assume that they are running because they're being machine-gunned. What you see is determined largely by what you hear, you can make many experiments, for example I've taken one of these Danger...James Bond...Man from Uncle programs and made a recording of it, then I shut off the sound track and used that sound track with another program, a similar program, and let someone watch it, they won't be able to tell the difference, you won't be able to make them believe that this is not the sound track that goes with that particular image track. Or you take one politician and record his speech and substitute it for another's. Of course no one knows the difference; there isn't that much difference.

Q : In making up a text out of various materials, what is the importance of points of intersection? Starting with this material, how do the "sequences" and "rhythms" organize themselves?

A : The points of intersection are very important certainly. In cutting up you will get a point of intersection where the new material that you have intersects with what is there already in some very precise way, and then you start from there. As to the sequences and rhythms organizing themselves, well, they don't. The cut-ups will give you new material but they won't tell you what to do with it.

Q : Have you tried enlarging on tape-recorder techniques with, say, some kind of computer?

A : Yes. This can be done on a computer. I have a very good friend, Ian Somerville, who is a computer programmer who says it is quite possible though very complicated. Certainly a computer can do any degree of cutting up or rearranging of materials that you put into it.

Q : But you haven't experimented with it?

A : To some extent, yes. Brion Gysin took some of his permutated poems and put them on a computer. Five words

I think runs to about sixty-four pages. All the possible permutations of it.

Q : What do you usually record, what kind of things?

A : I haven't done much recording lately. I've been very busy with straight writing. But I have recorded all sorts of things...street sounds, music, parties, conversations...

Q : What is the important thing in music, when you use music?

A : Music is extremely important. The whole Moslem world is practically controlled by music. Certain music is played at certain times, and the association of music is one of the most powerful. John Cage and Earl Brown have carried the cut-up method much further in music than I have in writing.

Q : Do you try for one kind of music rather than another?

A : I've made a lot of street recordings in Morocco that include music. There's nothing special about that; it's just recording music that you want to hear.

Q : Do you think that the prejudice that exists against the cut-up method and its extension can be attributed to the fear of really penetrating into time and space?

A : Very definitely. The word of course is one of the most powerful instruments of control as exercised by the newspaper and images as well, there are both words and images in newspapers... Now if you start cutting these up and rearranging them you are breaking down the control system. Fear and prejudice are always dictated by the control system just as the church built up prejudice against heretics; it wasn't inherent in the population, it was dictated by the church which was in control at that time. This is something that threatens the position of the establishment of any establishment, and therefore they will oppose it, will condition people to fear and reject or ridicule it.

Q : Is the ability "to see what is in front of us" a way of escaping from the image-prison which surrounds us?

A : Very definitely, yes. But this is an ability which very few people have, and fewer and fewer as time passes. For one thing, because of the absolute barrage of images to which we are subjected so that we become blunted. Remember that a hundred years ago there were relatively few images, and people living in a more simplified environment, a farm environment, encounter very few images and they see those quite clearly. But if you're absolutely bombarded with images from passing trucks and cars and televisions and newspapers, you become blunted and this makes a permanent haze in front of your eyes, you can't see anything.

Q : When you say that when you're in a world of simple images you see them more clearly, what do you mean by clearly?

A : There's nothing between them and the image. A farmer really sees his cows, he really sees what's in front of him quite clearly, it isn't a question of familiarity, it's a question of something being between you and the image, so that you can't see it. And as I say, this continual barrage of images makes haze over everything, like walking around in smog, we don't see anything.

I don't say that he has any sort of mystical identification with the cow but he's aware whether there's anything wrong with the cow, all sorts of things about the cow relative to how the cow is useful to him, and fits into his environment.

Q : Is the introduction of what you call "the message of resistance" the most important thing in the montage? Why?

A : Well, yes, I would say it's a very important factor in the montage because it does tend to break down the principal instruments of control which are word and image and to some extent to nullify them.

Q : *Your books are rarely obscure or hard to understand, and you have mentioned to me in conversation a desire to become even more clear. Is the concern for clarity consistent with a still vaster exploration of the infinite possibilities offered by your literary methods?*

A : When people speak of clarity in writing they generally mean plot, continuity, beginning middle and end, adherence to a "logical" sequence. But things don't happen in logical sequence and people don't think in logical sequence. Any writer who hopes to approximate what actually occurs in the mind and body of his characters cannot confine himself to such an arbitrary structure as "logical" sequence. Joyce was accused of being unintelligible and he was presenting only one level of cerebral events: conscious sub-vocal speech. I think it is possible to create multilevel events and characters that a reader could comprehend with his entire organic being.

Q : *You say that tape-recorder and cinema techniques can alter or falsify reality. How is this done?*

A : We think of the past as being there unchangeable. Actually the past is ours to shape and change as we will. Two men talk. Two men sitting under a tree worn smooth by others who sat there before or after time switched the track through a field of little white flowers. If no recording of the conversation is made, it exists only in the memory of the two actors. Suppose I make a recording of the conversation, alter and falsify the recording, and play the altered recording back to the two actors. If my alterations have been skillfully and plausibly applied (Yes... Mr B might well have said just that) the two actors will remember the altered recording.

Take a talking picture of you walking out in the morning to buy cigarettes and the papers. Run it back, you remember everything that happened, there it is on screen and muttering off the sound track... Now I can make you remember something that didn't happen by splicing it in. A truck passed just then: there it is on the screen, spliced in for you to remember. Always need a peg to hang it on. Well I plant a truck passed just then and what's so strange about that? Nothing, except it didn't pass just then, it passed a year ago and what more logical than said truck hitting a woman on a Paris corner three years later?

"I wonder if the old cow died or not," he said dazedly as the medics led him away. You see what I mean once you have a truck on set with Larry the Lorry at the wheel down Canal Street with no brakes blood and tennis shoes all over the street a limp foot dangles or say I splice in a little duffer asks you for the time it happens funny I didn't remember till now. Well once that little man who wasn't there is there on set he might well ship out a stiletto and assassinate the French Consul once the hole in reality is made and doubt consumed all the facts of history riddled with retroactive inserts all files and records of whatever nature to be immediately destroyed by order of the Emergency Sanitation Department documents are forgeries by nature before or after it is obvious.

Q : To what extent can this "new mythology," this new framework of associations and images, affect the awareness of the reader, and make him move about in space and time?

A : That would depend entirely on the reader, how open he is to new experience, and how able he is to move out of his own frame of reference. Of course most people are only able to give a very small fraction of their attention to what they read—to anything they're doing—because of their various compulsive preoccupations, and with just a tenth of their attention on something they don't move very far. Others are able to apply much more attention.

Q : Your characters are engulfed in a whirlwind of infernal happenings. They are bogged in the substance of the book. Is there a possible way to salvation for them?

A : I object to the word salvation as having a messianic Christian connotation, of final resolution... I don't feel that my characters, or the books in which they appear, are reflecting a mood of despair. Actually, in many ways they're in the tradition of the picaresque novel. It's a question of your interpretation of "infernal happenings," some people have much more tolerance for unusual happenings than others. People in small towns are absolutely appalled by some very slight change, whereas people in large cities are very much less upset by change, and if riots go on and on and on people are going to take them as a matter of course; they're already doing it.

Q : Do free men exist in your books?

A : Free men don't exist in anyone's books, because they are the author's creations. I would say that free men don't exist on this planet at this time, because they don't exist in human bodies, by the mere fact of being in a human body you're controlled by all sorts of biologic and environmental necessities.

Q : You often use silence as a device of terror, a "virus," as you call it, which breaks down characters into meaningless ciphers. What does this silence represent?

A : I don't think of silence as being a device of terror at all. In fact, quite the contrary. Silence is only frightening to people who are compulsively verbalizing. As you know they have these sense-withdrawal chambers and immersion chambers; there's one at the University of Oklahoma. Well, they put Marines in there, and they'd be absolutely out of their minds in about ten minutes, they could not endure silence and solitude because of the inner contradictions which words cover; but Gerald Heard got in there with a full dose of LSD and stayed three hours. Personally I find nothing upsetting about silence at all. In fact it can't get too quiet for me. I would say that silence is only a device of terror for compulsive verbalizers. . .

Q : *Is your interest in Maya civilization connected with the expansion of consciousness which you try to stimulate in your reader?*

CONTROL

A : The ancient Mayans possessed one of the most precise and hermetic control calendars ever hsed on this planet, a calendar that in effect controlled what the populace did thought and felt on any given day. A study of this model system throws light on modern methods of control. Knowledge of the calendar was the monopoly of a priestly caste who maintained their position with minimal police and military force. The priests had to start with a very accurate calendar for the tropical year consisting of 365 days divided into 18 months of 20 days and a final period of 5 days, the "Ouab days" which were considered especially unlucky and in consequence turned out to be so. An accurate calendar was essential to the foundation and maintenance of the priest's power. The Mayans were almost entirely dependent on the maize crop and the method of agriculture employed was slash and burn. Brush was cut down, allowed to dry and then burned. The corn was planted with a planting stick. The Mayans had no plows and no domestic animals capable of pulling a plow. Since the top soil is shallow and a stratum of lime-stone lies six inches under the surface plows are not func-tional in this area and the slash and burn method is used to the present day. Slash and burn cultivation depends

on exact timing. The brush must be cut and given time
to dry before the rains start. Miscalculation of a few days
can lose a year's crop. In addition to the yearly calendar
which regulated agricultural operations there was a sacred
almanac of 260 days. This ceremonial calendar governed
13 festivals of 20 days each. The ceremonial calendar
rolled through the year like a wheel and consequently the
festivals occurred at different dates each year but always
in the same sequence. The festivals consisted of religious
ceremonies, music, feasts, sometimes human sacrifice. Ac-
cordingly the priests could calculate into the future or the
past exactly what the populace would be doing hearing
seeing on a given date. This alone would have enabled
them to predict the future or reconstruct the past with
considerable accuracy since they could determine what
conditioning would be or had been applied on any given
date to a population which for many years remained in
hermetic seclusion protected by impassable mountains and
jungles from the waves of invaders who swept down the
central plateau of Mexico. There is every reason to infer
the existence of a third secret calendar which referred to
conditioning in precise sequence applied to the populace
under cover of the festivals very much as a stage magician
uses patter and spectacle to cover movements which
would otherwise be apparent to the audience. There are
many ways in which such conditioning can be effected the
simplest being waking suggestion which is fully explained
in a later context. Briefly, waking suggestion is a technique
for implanting verbal or visual suggestions which take
direct effect on the autonomic nervous system because the
subject's conscious attention is directed somewhere else,
in this case on the overt content of the festivals. (Waking
suggestion is not to be confused with subliminal suggestion which is suggestion below the level of conscious
awareness.) So the priests could calculate what the populace saw and heard on a given day and also what suggestions

were secretly implanted on that day. To obtain some idea of the secret calendar consider the Reactive Mind as postulated by L. Ron Hubbard the founder of Scientology. Mr Hubbard describes the R.M. as an ancient instrument of control designed to stultify and limit the potential for action in a constructive or destructive direction. The precise content of the R.M. as set forth in his formulation is considered confidential material since it can cause illness and upsets so I will limit myself to general considerations without giving the exact phrases used: The R.M. consists of consequential, sequential and contradictory propositions that have command value at the automatic level of behavior, quite as automatic and involuntary as the metabolic commands that regulate rate of heartbeats, digestion, balance of chemical constituents in the blood stream, brain waves. The regulatory center of the autonomic nervous system which controls bodily processes and metabolism is the hypothalamus in the back brain. Undoubtedly the hypothalamus is the neurological intersection point where the R.M. is implanted. The R.M. may be described as an artificially constructed and highly disadvantageous regulatory system grafted onto the natural regulatory center. The R.M. as expounded by Mr Hubbard is of considerable antiquity antedating all modern languages and yet manifesting itself through all modern languages. Consequently it must refer to a *symbol system*. And except for the intervention of Bishop Landa we could infer by analogy what this symbol system consisted of since all control systems are basically similar. Bishop Landa collected all the Mayan books he could lay hands on, a stack of them six feet high, and burned the lot. To date only three authenticated Mayan codices have turned up that survived this barbarous action.

Mr Hubbard logically postulates that the R.M. commands take effect because they relate to actual goals, needs, conditions of those effected. A consequential command is a command that one must obey in consequence of having been born: "to be here in a human body." A sequential command follows from this basic proposition: "to seek food, shelter, sexual satisfaction," "to exist in relation to other human bodies." Contradictory commands are two commands that contradict each other given at the same time. "TENSHUN!" The soldier automatically stiffens to the command. "AT EASE!" The soldier automatically relaxes. Now imagine a captain who strides into the barracks snapping "TENSHUN" from one side of his face and "AT EASE" from the other. (Quite possible to do this with dubbing techniques.) The attempt to obey two flatly contradictory commands at once both of which have a degree of command value at the automatic level disorients the subject. He may react with rage, apathy, anxiety, even collapse. Another example: I give the command "sit down" and when the command is obeyed promptly the subject receives a reward. If it is not obeyed promptly he receives a severe electric shock. When he has been conditioned to obey I add the command "stand up" and condition him to obey this command in precisely the same way. Now I give both commands simultaneously. The result may well be complete collapse as Pavlov's dogs collapsed when given contradictory signals at such short intervals that their nervous systems could not adjust. The aim of these commands from the viewpoint of a control system is to limit and confine. All control units employ such commands. For contradictory commands to have force the subject must have been conditioned to obey both commands automatically and the commands must relate to his actual goals. "TENSHUN" "AT EASE" "SIT DOWN" "STAND UP" are arbitrary commands tenuously connected to any basic goal of the subject—(of course "TENSHUN" relates to the goal to be a good soldier or at least to stay out of the guardhouse which gives the command what strength it has)—Consider

another pair of commands that contradict each other: "to
make a good impression" "to make an awful impression."
This relates to much more basic goals. Everyone wants to
make a good impression. His self-regard, livelihood, sexual
satisfaction depend on making a good impression. Why
then does the subject when he is trying most desperately
to make a good impression make the worst impression
possible? Because he also has the goal to make a bad impression which operates on an involuntary automatic level.
This self-destructive goal is such a threat to his being that
he reacts against it. He may be conscious or partially conscious of the negative goal but he cannot confront it
directly. The negative goal forces him to react. The Reactive Mind consists of goals so repulsive or frightening to
the subject that he compulsively reacts against them and
it is precisely this reaction that keeps these negative goals
in operation. Negative goals are implanted by fear. Consider a pair of contradictory commands that were undoubtedly used in some form by the Mayan priests: "to
rebel stridently" "to submit meekly." Every time a worker
nerved himself to rebel the goal to submit was activated
causing him to assert rebellion more and more stridently
thus activating more and more compulsively the goal to
submit. So he trembles stammers and collapses before an
authority figure that he consciously despises. No exercise
of so-called will power affects these automatic reactions.
The goal to submit was implanted by a threat so horrible
that he could not confront it, and the Mayan secret books
obviously consisted of such horrific pictures. The few that
have survived bear witness to this. Men are depicted turning into centipedes, crabs, plants. Bishop Landa was so
appalled by what he saw that his own reactive mind dictated his vandalous act. Like his modern counterparts
who scream for censorship and book burning he did not
take account of the fact that any threat clearly seen and
confronted loses force. The Mayan priests took care that

the populace did not see the books. Mr Hubbard's R.M. contains about 300 items. Some are commands arranged in pairs, some are visual representations. Using the R.M. as a model—and the Mayan system must have been quite similar—postulate that during a ceremonial month of 20 days four items were repeated or represented 20 times on the first day, 4 more items 20 times on the second day and so on 80 items for the 20-day month. The next 20-day month of the sacred almanac 80 more items until the items were exhausted after which they were repeated in precisely the same sequence thus constituting a secret calendar. The priests then could calculate precisely what reactive commands had been or would be restimulated on any date past or future and these calculations enabled them to reconstruct the past or predict the future with considerable accuracy. They were dealing from a stacked deck. Calculations of past and future calendar juxtapositions took up a good deal of their time and they were more concerned with the past than the future. There are calculations that go back 400,000,000 years. These probings into the remote past may be interpreted as an assertion that the calendars always existed and always will exist. (All control systems claim to reflect the immutable laws of the universe.) These calculations must have looked like this:

year, month, day of the 365-day calendar which was calculated from 5 Ahua 8 Cumhu

a mythical date when time began

year month and day of the sacred almanac or ceremonial calendar

year month and day of the secret calendar

Mayan students have succeeded in deciphering dates in the 365-day calendar. Lacking cross references comparable to the Rosetta Stone much of the writing remains unsolved. If we interpret the writing as oriented toward control we can postulate that all the inscriptions refer to dates and the events, ceremonies, suggestions, pictures and planetary juxtapositions correlated with dates. Any control system depends on precise timing. A picture or suggestion may be quite innocuous at one time and devastating at another. For example "to make a splendid impression" "to make an awful impression" may have no effect on somebody when he is not in a competitive context. Same man bucking for lieutenant bars or apprentice priest can be reliably washed out by the same pair of contradictory commands, brought into restimulation.

This seemingly hermetic control calendar broke down even before the Aztecs invaded Yucatan and long before the arrival of the Spaniards. All control systems work on punishment-reward. When punishment overbalances reward, when the masters have no rewards left to give, revolts occur. The continual demands for forced labor on the temples and stellae coupled with a period of famine may have been the precipitating factor. Or possibly some forgotten Bolívar revealed the content of the secret books. In any case the workers rebelled, killed the priests and defaced the stellae and temples as symbols of enslavement.

Now translate the Mayan control calendar into modern terms. The mass media of newspapers, radio, television, magazines form a ceremonial calendar to which all citizens are subjected. The "priests" wisely conceal themselves behind masses of contradictory data and vociferously deny that they exist. Like the Mayan priests they can reconstruct the past and predict the future on a statistical basis through manipulation of media. It is the daily press preserved in newspaper morgues that makes detailed reconstruction of past dates possible. How can the modern priests predict seemingly random future events? Start with the many factors in mass media that can be controlled and predicted:

1. Layout: the format of newspapers and magazines can be decided in advance. The TV programs to be used in

juxtaposition with news broadcasts can be decided in advance.

2. *The news to be played up and the news to be played down:* 10 years ago in England drug arrests were four-line back-page items. Today they are front-page headlines.

3. *Editorials and letters to the editor:* The letters published are of course selected in accordance with preconceived policy.

4. *Advertisements:* So the modern ceremonial calendar is almost as predictable as the Mayan. What about the secret calendar? Any number of reactive commands can be inserted in advertisements, editorials, newspaper stories. Such commands are implicit in the layout and juxtaposition of items. Contradictory commands are an integral part of the modern industrial environment: Stop. Go. Wait here. Go there. Come in. Stay out. Be a man. Be a woman. Be white. Be black. Live. Die. Be your real self. Be somebody else. Be a human animal. Be a superman. Yes. No. Rebel. Submit. RIGHT. WRONG. Make a splendid impression. Make an awful impression. Sit down. Stand up. Take your hat off. Put your hat on. Create. Destroy. Live now. Live in the future. Live in the past. Obey the law. Break the law. Be ambitious. Be modest. Accept. Reject. Plan ahead. Be spontaneous. Decide for yourself. Listen to others. Talk. SILENCE. Save money. Spend money. Speed up. Slow down. This way. That way. Right. Left. Present. Absent. Open. Closed. Entrance. Exit. IN. OUT, etc., round the clock. This creates a vast pool of statistical newsmakers. It is precisely uncontrollable automatic reactions that make news. The controllers know what reactive commands they are going to restimulate and in consequence they know what will happen. Contradictory suggestion is the basic formula of the daily press: "Take drugs everybody is doing it." "Drug-taking is WRONG." Newspapers spread violence, sex, drugs, then come on with the old RIGHT WRONG FAMILY

CHURCH AND COUNTRY sound. It is wearing very
thin. The modern control calendar is breaking down.
Punishment now overbalances reward in the so-called
"permissive" society, and young people no longer want
the paltry rewards offered them. Rebellion is world-wide.
The present controllers have an advantage which the
Mayan priests did not have: an overwhelming arsenal of
weapons which the rebels cannot hope to obtain or duplicate. Clubs and spears can be produced by anyone. Tanks,
planes, battleships, heavy artillery and nuclear weapons
are a monopoly of those in power. As their psychological
domination weakens modern establishments are relying
more and more on this advantage and now maintain their
position by naked force—(How permissive is the "permissive society?")—Yet the advantage of weaponry is not
so overwhelming as it appears. To implement weapons
the controllers need soldiers and police. These guardians
must be kept under reactive control. Hence the controllers
must rely on people who are always stupider and more
degraded by the conditioning essential to their suppressive
function.

Techniques exist to erase the Reactive Mind and
achieve a complete freedom from past conditioning and
immunity against such conditioning in the future. Scientology processing accomplishes this. Erasure of the R.M.
is carried out on the E Meter a very sensitive reaction
tester developed by Mr Hubbard. If an R.M. item reads
on the E Meter the subject is still reacting to it. When
an item ceases to read he is no longer reacting to it. It
may be necessary to run the entire R.M. hundreds of
times to effect complete erasure. But it will erase. The
method works. I can testify to that through my own
experience. It takes time, at least two months of training
8 hours a day to learn how to use the E Meter and how
to run the material. It is expensive, about 3,000 dollars
for the training and processing that leads to erasure of

the Reactive Mind. A reconstruction of the symbol system that must underlie the Reactive Mind would open the way for more precise and speedy erasure.

Two recent experiments indicate the possibility of mass deconditioning. In one experiment volunteers were wired to an encephalographic unit that recorded their brain waves. When alpha brain waves, which are correlated with a relaxed state of mind and body appeared on screen the subject was instructed to maintain this state as long as possible. After some practice alpha waves could be produced at will. The second experiment is more detailed and definitive: *Herald Tribune*, Jan. 31, 1969: "U.S. scientist demonstrated that animals can learn to control such automatic responses as heart rate, blood pressure, glandular secretions and brain waves in response to rewards and punishments. The psychologist is Doctor N.E. Miller. He says that his findings upset the traditional thinking that the autonomic nervous system which controls the workings of the heart, digestive system and other internal organs is completely involuntary. Doctor Miller and his co-workers were able to teach animals to increase or decrease the amount of saliva they produced, raise or lower their blood pressure, increase or decrease their intestinal contractions, stomach activity and urinary output and change their brain wave patterns using as a reward direct electrical stimulation of the so-called reward areas of the brain when the desired response occurred. Rats were able to learn to raise or lower their heart rates by 20 percent in 90 minutes of training. Retesting showed that they remembered their lessons well, Doctor Miller said." In what way does this experiment differ from the experiments by which Pavlov demonstrated the conditioned reflex? I quote from *Newsweek*, February 10, 1969: "Until now most psychologists believed that the autonomic nervous system could be trained only by the the advancement of knowledge. Mr Hubbard's overtly fascist utterances... (China is the real danger to world peace, Scientology is protecting the home, the church, the family, decent morals...(no wife swapping)...national boundaries, the concept of RIGHT AND WRONG.) against evil free-thinking psychiatrists can hardly recommend him to the militant students. Certainly it is time for Scientology to come out in plain English on one side or the other if they expect the trust and support of young people. Which side are you on Hubbard which side are you on?

Q : *You write: "I am a recorder... I do not pretend to impose 'story,' plot, or continuity." Is it possible?*

A : I can only answer that question by saying that when I said that I was perhaps going a bit far. One tries not to impose story plot or continuity artificially but you do have to compose the materials, you can't just dump down a jumble of notes and thoughts and considerations and expect people to read it.

Q : *"Words—at least as we use them—tend to hide non-physical experience from us." Once one has removed the barriers which Aristotle, Descartes and Co. put in the way, is this "non-physical experience" parallel to (i.e., interrelated with) physical experience? Is every physical experience therefore undergone on various levels?*

A : Yes, very definitely. For example, so-called psychic experiences are experienced insofar as one experiences them at all through the physical senses. People see or hear ghosts, feel various emanations, presences, etc.

Q : *Do you think that classical philosophical thought has had a damaging effect on human life?*

A : Well, it's completely outmoded, as Korzybski, the man who developed general semantics, has pointed out, the Aristotelian "either-or"—something is either this or that

—is one of the great errors of Western thinking, because it's no longer true at all. That sort of thinking does not even correspond to what we now know about the physical universe.

Q : Why has it been accepted for so long?

A : There are certain formulas, word-locks, which will lock up a whole civilization for a thousand years. Now another thing is Aristotle's *is* of identity: this *is* a chair. Now, whatever it may be, it's not a chair, it's not the word chair, it's not the label chair. The idea that the label is the thing leads to all sorts of verbal arguments, when you're dealing with labels, and think you're dealing with objects. Yes, I would agree emphatically that Aristotle, Descartes, and all that way of thinking is extremely stultifying and doesn't correspond even to what we know about the physical universe, and particularly disastrous in that it still guides the whole academic world. They were bitterly opposed to Korzybski and his general semantics, which would seem to be an obvious consideration—that labels are not the things they stand for, that when you're arguing about labels, when you're talking about things like democracy, communism and fascism that have no clear-cut references, no clear-cut thing to which they refer, you're not talking about anything.

Q : Are people, sprawled in what you call their "garbage cans of words," still capable of feeling the violence of your words, or is it necessary to resort to physical violence to get them out of their garbage cans?

A : I would say that generally speaking, if somebody's really tied up in words, they will not experience anything from my books at all except automatic disapproval. It probably is necessary to resort to physical violence, which is happening everywhere. There doesn't seem to be any alternative, since the establishments won't change their basic premises.

Q : Do you think any means, including physical violence, will actually change people who are completely tied up?

A : The point of physical violence is that it can displace them. People who are completely verbal, like judges and politicians just won't change their premises, and of course, if people absolutely refuse to change their premises and the development nonetheless takes place, they're finally displaced by some violence or disaster.

Q : Where does humor fit into the scheme of your work?

A : Well, I think of my work as being, I won't say largely humorous, but certainly having a considerable element of humor.

Q : The hell which you describe, and the accusations which you make, imply their opposites and their expiations; so they might be taken as offering man a way out. It has been said that you are a great moralist; what do you think?

A : Yes, I would say perhaps too much so. There are any number of things that could be done in the present situation. The point is that they are not being done, none of them are being done. And, I don't know whether there's any possibility of their being done, given the extent of stupidity and bad intentions on the part of the people in power. You're running up against a wall to even point this out; but all sorts of things can be done that would alleviate the present situation. Perfectly simple things in terms of present techniques. What it amounts to is breaking down three basic formulas: one is the formula of a nation. You draw a line around a piece of ground and say this is a nation. Then you have to have police, customs control, armies, and eventually trouble with the people on the other side of the line. That is one formula; and any variation of that formula is going to come to the same thing. The UN is going to get nowhere. What are they doing? They're creating more of

these bloody nations all the time. That's one formula.
The next formula is of course the family. And nations are
simply an extension of the family. And (possibly this is
a matter for future techniques) the whole present method
of birth and reproduction. Those are basic formulas that
need to be broken down.

Q : You have some rather far-reaching changes in mind?

A : Yes, certainly, you have to be very far-reaching—there
are ways of breaking down the family, of course the
Chinese are on the way to it. They're the only people
who've done anything about it. The Russians said they
were going to and didn't. And they still guard the same
old bourgeois family.

Q : What did you mean when you wrote: "A certain use
of words and images can lead to silence"?

A : I think I was being over-optimistic. I doubt if the
whole problem of words can ever be solved in terms of
itself.

Q : Wright Morris called Naked Lunch a hemorrhage of
the imagination. Would you take that as a compliment?

A : I frankly wouldn't know how to take it.

Q : I assume he meant a fatal hemorrhage.

A : Hemorrhages do not necessarily lead to death. I
wouldn't take it really as a compliment. What do you
think of there? You think of a cerebral hemorrhage, of
someone with fuses blowing out in his brain. No, I don't
take it as a compliment at all.

Q : Who is Wright Morris?

A : I have no idea, never heard of him.

Q : You set yourself apart from the postwar American
novel which does not really know what imagination

means. American writers suppose that the public is interested only in real facts, in the most material sense of the word. Your books are widely read in the United States; perhaps they describe a universe which is at the same time imaginary and real.

A : Well, yes, I think so. So many novels now really come under the head of journalism, they try accurately to describe just what people actually do. It's rather journalism and anthropology than writing. It seems to me that a novel should rework that, not just dump a lot of purely factual observations on the reader.

Q : What do you suppose accounts for the attachment of American writers to material reality?

A : Hum, well, of course we had the social consciousness novels of the 1930's, and that tradition is still quite strong. The idea that a novel should deal with reality, with people, with real problems, and particularly with social problems of one sort or another, which actually is not too far from the novels of Zola. It's a relatively old tradition. I don't think it's confined at all to American writers.

Q : What is your relation to the Beat movement, with which you associate yourself? What is the literary importance of this movement?

A : I don't associate myself with it at all, and never have, either with their objectives or their literary style. I have some close personal friends among the Beat movement: Jack Kerouac and Allen Ginsberg and Gregory Corso are all close personal friends of many years standing, but were not doing at all the same thing, either in writing or in outlook. You couldn't really find four writers more different, more distinctive. It's simply a matter of juxtaposition rather than any actual association of literary styles or overall objectives. The literary importance of this movement? I would say that the literary importance of the

Beatnik movement is perhaps not as obvious as its sociological importance. . .it really has transformed the world
and populated the world with Beatniks. It has broken
down all sorts of social barriers and become a worldwide
phenomenon of terrific importance. The Beatniks will go
to someplace like North Africa, and they contact the
Arabs on a level that seems to me to be more fundamental
than the old Arab-speaking settlers, who are still thinking
in T.E. Lawrence terms. It's an important sociological
phenomenon, and, as I say, worldwide.

Q : When you say they communicate on a fundamental
level, do you mean that all people all over the world share
certain fundamental levels?

A : Well, partly. . .they contact the Arabs on the subject
of drugs—that is, the subject of kif—which is an important contact. How do you contact people? After all, you
contact them on certain fundamental levels, on sex, habits, drugs. But more than that, they're coordinated with
pop music, with a way of dressing, a way of life; it is something that has influenced the youth of the world, not only
in Western countries but in Eastern countries as well.

Q : Open-mindedness, really; is that it? The thing that your
European settler lacks?

A : Yes. The old settlers are stuck back in the 19th century.
"These people are quite charming really but of course
we'll never understand them not really." Then some anecdote to illustrate the quaintness of Arabs and how different their thinking is from ours. They see the Arabs from
outside as observers with preconceptions about how Arabs
think. The Beatniks do not have this folkloric viewpoint.
They assume that the Arab way of thinking is not basically different from their own and make direct contact.
The old settlers create a gap by assuming that it exists.

Q : What do you think of Mailer? Bellow? Capote?

A : Very difficult question... You have to be careful what you say about your literary colleagues. I am not too much of a reader, unfortunately, and when I read I tend to read science fiction, so I can't really speak with too much authority. I've read Mailer's early work *The Naked and the Dead*, which I thought was a very fine novel; Bellow's *Dangling Man*, which I enjoyed. I thought that Capote's earlier work showed extraordinary and very unusual talent, which I can't say for this *In Cold Blood*, which it seems to me could have been written by any staff editor on *The New Yorker*.

Q : American writers, like most others, seem particularly interested in judging, supporting, or condemning each other, each one having the impression of being in possession of the truth. How do you feel about this sort of thing?

A : Well, this has always been going on, this cliquishness of writers. I think its furthest development was reached in France, with the surrealists all attacking other writers. Breton spent a great deal of his time writing abusive letters to other writers... I think literary arguments are a terrific waste of time, myself. I don't care to get engaged in polemics and manifestoes and condemnations of other writers or schools of writing.

Q : Have there been writers in the conventional, "classic" tradition who have succeeded in escaping from the imprisonment of words?

A : Well, escaping from the imprisonment of words, that's a little bit equivocal. I think there are certain writers in the conventional classic tradition who have produced extraordinary effects with words which sometimes went beyond words. One of my favorite writers is Joseph Conrad, who is certainly in the classic tradition; and he's done some quite remarkable books in collaboration with Ford Madox Ford, which are very little read now. I'd mention *The Inheritors* and *Romance*, and there are passages

where he does seem to be escaping from words, or going
beyond words, in a quite conventional, quite classic narrative form.

Q : Finnegans Wake *is generally regarded as a magnificent
literary dead end. What is your opinion?*

A : I think *Finnegans Wake* rather represents a trap into
which experimental writing can fall when it becomes
purely experimental. I would go so far with any given
experiment and then come back; that is, I am coming
back now to write purely conventional straightforward
narrative. But applying what I have learned from the
cut-up and the other techniques to the problem of conventional writing. It's simply if you go too far in one
direction, you can never get back, and you're out there in
complete isolation, like this anthropologist who spent
the last 20 years of his life on the sweet-potato controversy, which was whether the sweet potato was native
to the New World, or whether it floated over from Indonesia, or whether it floated the other way. This went
on for 20 years. . .and he would write acrimonious letters
to various very specialized anthropological publications
attacking the people who opposed his views on the
sweet-potato controversy; but I forget which way he
thought the sweet potato went!

Q : *Beckett? Genet?*

A : Beckett and Genet I both admire without reservation.
They're both incredible writers, I think. And, of course,
Genet is not, nor does he pretend to be, a verbal in-
novator. He is in the classic tradition, and there is another writer who, using the classic tradition, certainly
seems to escape the imprisonment of words and to achieve
things that you think could not be achieved in words.

Q : *What is your impression of the commitments of writers
who hope to achieve, by political activity, a remedy or an
improvement for our civilization? Do you think that this
kind of activity tends to limit one's creative capacity, or
perhaps reveals its limits?*

A : Well, I think overcommitment to political objectives definitely does limit one's creative capacity; you tend to become a polemicist rather than a writer. Being very dubious of politics myself, and against the whole concept of a nation, which politics presupposes, it does seem to me something of a dead end, at least for myself. I suppose that there are writers who really derive their inspiration from political commitments and who sometimes achieve good results: Malraux is an example. In his early work, like *Man's Fate*, which definitely grew out of his political commitments, and yet was a very fine novel. ·

Q : The literary techniques to Raymond Roussel attempt to enmesh the writer in a system; yours tend on the other hand to free him. What might be the importance of a technique to a writer?

A : Well, those can be interesting experiments, some of them will work and some of them won't. Some of these, you can say he's done a very interesting experiment, and it's quite unreadable. I know I've done a lot of that myself. I've done writing that I thought was interesting, experimentally, but simply not readable.

Q : Do you need the reader?

A : A novelist is essentially engaged in creating character. He needs the reader in that he hopes that some of his readers will turn into his characters. He needs them as vessels, on which he writes. The question frequently asked of a writer is: "Would you write if you were on a desert island and no one would ever read it?"

I would say certainly, yes, I would write, in order to create characters. My characters are quite as real to me as so-called real people; which is one reason why I'm not subject to what is known as loneliness. I have plenty of company.

two

Prisoners of the earth come out

Q : We spoke of images and words which hold man prisoner, and which are the logical outcome of a vast system of annihilation. The next step would be to locate the various springs of the mechanism, and for a start, its origin. How do you see it?

A. : Image and word are the instruments of control used by the daily press and by such news magazines as *Time, Life, Newsweek*, and their English and Continental counterparts. Of course, an instrument can be used without knowledge of its fundamental nature or its origins. To get to the origin we must examine the instruments themselves; that is, the actual nature of word and image. Research along these lines is discouraged by those who use word and image as instruments of control. So we do not know what a word is or what an image is. The study of hieroglyphic languages shows us that a word is an image ...the written word is an image. However, there is an important difference between a hieroglyphic and a syllabic language. If I hold up a sign with the word "ROSE" written on it, and you read that sign, you will be forced to repeat the word "ROSE" to yourself. If I show you a picture of a rose you do not have to repeat the word. You can register the image in silence. A syllabic language forces you to verbalize in auditory patterns. A hieroglyphic language does not. I think that anyone who is interested to find out the precise relationship between word and image should study a simplified hieroglyphic script. Such a study would tend to break down the automatic verbal reaction to a word. It is precisely these automatic reactions to words themselves that enable those who manipulate words to control thought on a mass scale.

Q : What is the importance of power, in all its forms, in the machinery of destruction?

A : The exercise of power for power's sake is precisely the machine of destruction. This would seem to be something we have had throughout history, and in a sense this is true. The difference is a matter of degree. Old-fashioned power, the generalissimo shooting a provincial governor across his desk, has self-limiting goals, and at least a measure of self-preservation. To confuse this old-style power with the manifestation of control madness we see now on this planet is to confuse a disappearing wart with an exploding cancer. You might as well expect a measure of moderation, or at least self-preservation, from the virus of rabies which dies when you do, mission accomplished. What we see now is power exercised for purely destructive purposes. Whether they know it or not, the present controllers are bent on annihilation.

Q : And what of money, ownership, property?

A : Vested interest of power and/or money is perhaps the most potent factor standing in the way of freedom for the individual. New discoveries and products are suppressed because they threaten vested interests. The medical profession is suppressing Reich's orgone accumulator and his discoveries relative to the use and dangers of orgonic energy. They are suppressing Dianetics and Scientology discovered by Mr L. Ron Hubbard. They are suppressing the use of massive doses of Vitamin E for the prevention of heart disease, the use of massive doses of Vitamin A for curing the common cold. (I have used this simple remedy for thirty years and it works. Everyone I have passed it on to has found that it works either to abort or modify the course of a cold. At the first soreness in the throat which presages the onslaught of a common cold you take 500,000 units of Vitamin A. Vitamin A alone. Not Vitamin C which is quite worthless for a cold. At one time I had thought to market this remedy but was told it could not be marketed because the American Medical Association is opposed to self-medication. The AMA is opposed to self-medication if it works.) The medical profession is suppressing the use of apomorphine for the treatment of alcoholism and drug addiction and for the general regulation of disturbed metabolism. The medical profession has a *vested interest in illness.* They suppress any discovery that strikes at the roots of illness.

The real-estate lobby has a vested interest in the housing shortage. They sabotage any attempt to provide good cheap housing. An example of this suppression is the Lustron house. A man named Lustron devised a prefabricated house of porcelain steel, with a layer of insulation in the middle. This house was termite-proof, rust-proof, age-proof. It would still be there a thousand years from now. Lustron planned to put this house out for five thousand dollars. He only manufactured a few hundred Lustron houses before he was forced out of business by the real-estate lobby. They blocked him from obtaining the necessary materials.

The Tucker car is another example: Tucker devised a car so much better than any car on the market it would have forced big motor companies to change their dies and produce a car of equal performance. Since they could sell the inferior cars they were already set up to produce, it was cheaper and easier to block Tucker... No materials! He lost 20,000,000 dollars and nearly went to jail. The Tucker car never hit the open market.

Other examples are the blocking of the ramie industry by the Duponts and other manufacturers of synthetic fabrics. Where are the bicycle helicopters we were supposed to have by now?

Where are the aluminium houses?

The police have a vested interest in criminality. The Narcotics Department has a vested interest in addiction. Politicians have a vested interest in nations. Army officers have a vested interest in war. Vested interest, whether operating through private, capital or official agencies, suppresses any discovery, product or way of thought that threatens its area of monopoly. The cold war is used as a pretext by both America and Russia to conceal and monopolize research confining knowledge to official agencies. It is no exaggeration to say that all important research is now top secret, until someone lets a rat out of the bag. Infrasound, for example: I quote from a *Sunday Times* article, April 16, 1967, "Acoustics," by Frank Dorsey, under the title "Joshua Knew a Thing or Two":

"The world is not noticeably short of lethal weapons, but a team of French scientists in Marseille is working on a death-ray machine designed to provide an entirely novel method of human destruction. The project began when the Electro-Acoustical laboratory moved into a new building three years ago. Staff complained of headache and nausea. Investigations began. Electromagnetic waves were suspected and eliminated. So were ultra-sound waves.

"At this point, one of the technicians got out an antique apparatus for detecting infrasound—that is, air vibrations which oscillate at less than ten vibrations a second, or 10 Hertz—(The human ear registers, as sound vibrations, from 16Hz to 20,000Hz) it had been used during the First World War to distinguish cannon fire and movement of trains too far off to be unscrambled by ears. I quickly identified the source of the unease: the giant ventilator of a factory next door. After changing the ventilator's frequency, the five-man team headed by Professor Vladimir Gavreau decided to find out more about the properties of infrasound."

As everyone knows, sound is a succession of waves in which the air is alternatively compressed and decompressed. Fast vibrations either go right through solid objects or bounce off them, usually doing relatively little harm even when very powerful. But slow vibration, below the hearing level, can create a sort of pendulum action, a reverberation in solid objects that quickly builds up to intolerable intensity. To study this phenomenon the team built a giant whistle, hooked to a compressed air hose. Then they turned on the air. Professor Gavreau says:

"Luckily, we were able to turn it off quickly. All of us were sick for hours. Everything in us was vibrating: stomach, heart, lungs. All the people in the other laboratories were sick too. They were very angry with us."

The first blast was audible only down to 190 Hz. It had an acoustical force of about 100 Watts, compared with one watt for a football referee's whistle. From then on the team worked at lowering the frequency, but carefully kept the power input down. A bigger whistle was built, measuring about five feet across. It emits a very low but audible tone, at about 37 Hz. If turned on full blast, it would develop 2000 Watts—and the building would fall down like the walls of Jericho before Joshua's trumpet. At the pressures used it has done no more than put cracks in the ceiling. The team has discovered that the wave length most dangerous to human life is 7 Hz. At 7 Hz, turned on very softly, one has a vague impression of sound, and a general feeling of discomfort. At 3.5 Hz, nothing can be heard directly but there is a curious incidental effect. Nearby sounds, such as air hissing into the pipe, take on a pulsing quality—at 3.5 pulsations a second. All sounds in the neighborhood seem to ululate rhythmically. The team has suffered from its experiments. Some of the invisible injuries appear to be persistent.

"It not only affects the ears," Professor Gavreau says, "but it works directly on the internal organs. There is a rubbing between the various organs because of a sort of resonance. It provokes an irritation so intense that for hours afterwards any low-pitched sound seems to echo through one's body."

In developing a military weapon, scientists intend to revert to a policeman's whistle form, perhaps as big as eighteen feet across, mount it on a truck and blow it with a fan turned by a small airplane engine. This weapon, they say, will give forth an all-destroying 10,000 acoustic watts. It could kill a man five miles away. There is one snag: at present, the machine is as dangerous to its operators as to the enemy. The team is working on a way to focus it. Various systems of baffles have been tried, but the most promising method appears to be propagation of a different and complementary sound a wave length backward from the machine. This changes the frequency of airwave length moving in that direction, thus protecting anyone to the rear.

There is, of course, a much simpler means of protection: turn the machine on from a safe distance.

This summary of Professor Vladimir Gavreau's experiments with infrasound is based on the Sunday Times article.

A much more comprehensive article has appeared in an American periodical, The National Enquirer, Vol. 42, No. 27, March 10, 1968. Professor Gavreau's discovery has been patented and anybody can obtain the plans and full description from the French patent office upon payment of two francs. Undoubtedly top secret projects are exploring the military potentials of infrasound. Since sub-lethal infrasound paralyzes the mental functions—(as Professor Gavreau put it "I could not add two and two")—well add two and two and you will see that infrasound is an ideal weapon against dissident elements within the establishment. It is to be hoped that hobbyists will obtain the plans and experiment. The materials necessary are cheap and easily obtained. Perhaps infrasound has therapeutic properties at low volume and borderline infrasound might add a new dimension to pop music. Another scientist who freely published his discoveries was Wilhelm Reich. He died in a federal prison. Most of you know something of Reich's experiments, discoveries and theories so I will not undertake a detailed rundown here. You can still buy Reich's books despite the book-burning carried out by the Pure Food and Drug pigs in emulation of their Nazi prototypes. I would like to draw attention to Reich's experiments with DOR—Deadly Orgone Radiation. DOR is produced by putting any radioactive material into an orgone accumulator. In Reich's experiments very small quantities of radioactive material were used. None the less the effect is described as "being hit on the head with a sledge hammer." One experimenter nearly died as a result of exposure. Very dilute exposure produces mental confusion, depression, anxiety and restlessness. Like infrasound DOR has a range from the almost imperceptible to the lethal. The experiments with DOR are fully described in *The Selected Writings* of Wilhelm Reich in the chapter entitled *Orgone Physics*. (This book published by Vision Press Limited, Saxone House, 74a, Regent Street, London is obtainable in the Indica Book Shop, 102, Southampton Row.) Anyone with a radium watch dial can duplicate these experiments. It seems that immunity to DOR is conveyed by gradient exposure. In fact the purpose of the DOR experiments was to find a means of conveying mass immunization to radiation sickness. As you know Reich's books and papers were burned, his experiments outlawed and he himself imprisoned. It is to say the least probable that top secret experiments with DOR are being carried out by official agencies. Experiments which offer any possibility of immunization to radiation sickness certainly deserve to be fully explored and widely publicized.

Mr L. Ron Hubbard, the founder of Dianetics and Scientology, has also been persecuted by the Pure Food and Drug Department. To date Mr Hubbard has refused to publish his advanced discoveries. There is every indication that the discoveries of Scientology are being used by the CIA and other official agencies. With these discoveries already in the worst possible hands it is to be hoped that Mr Hubbard will reserve his present policies.

To Mr Hubbard belongs the credit for making public a secret weapon used extensively by the Americans and the Russians in their dreary cold-war farce. This weapon is pain-drug hypnosis. Ordinary hypnosis cannot force the subject to act against his moral code or his own interests and survival. Pain-drug hypnosis can. The subject is drugged into unconsciousness, beaten in a way that will leave no mark—(telephone book, hard pillow)—and given suggestions. He will obey these suggestions without knowing that he has been drugged and subjected to pain-drug hypnosis. He will obey these suggestions however much they may conflict with his moral code or his interests. Even suicide can be so induced.

In the case of Reich and Hubbard discoveries have been suppressed by official agencies in all probability to mask secret experiments along the same lines.

A recent article in *Esquire* magazine written by a former CIA agent contains this anecdote: A man with photos of the Bay of Pigs was on the way to a newspaper office when the agent who was tailing him called a "special number" in Washington. "On the way to the newspaper office he was run down by a laundry truck." Not so easy to be sure of nailing someone on a walk across town after all people do look before crossing a street. I would venture the guess that he was pushed in front of the laundry truck by a laser. Lasers can move satellites in and out of orbit. They could push someone in front of a truck. Is this knowledge in the best hands?

Nine years ago in Amsterdam, I talked with a Dutch chemist who told me they had synthesized a drug infinitely more potent than LSD, and could not take the responsibility of testing this drug on human subjects, owing to the possibility of residual brain damage. Subsequently, I heard that the drug has now been released to "official agencies" in America. This may well be the "nonlethal nerve gas" being used in Vietnam. Recently I heard from someone connected with a laser research project conducted by the U.S. Navy: "They can actually send a thought." Some years ago, experiments in Norway indicated the possibility of activating speech patterns directly in the brain by means of an electromagnetic field. Hearing voices? The Black Box which develops positive ions, enabling anyone within its range to perform at a high level of efficiency without fatigue, was used by the U.S. Army and kept secret for ten years. Is it on the market yet?

Important research that could be used to free the human spirit is being monopolized by paltry intellects in the name of "National Security." What are you getting out of "national security"? The cold war is an essential factor in maintaining the establishment of the West and in Russia, and has all the marks of a deal under the table. Top secret classified research is not top secret because the Russians might find out about it. The Russians already know and in most cases are well ahead of the West. Top secret research is top secret because establishments do not want young people of the world to find out what they are doing.

Q : *The Lemur is an odd animal which you mention in* Naked Lunch. *What does it symbolize?*

A : It would seem that at one time there were many humanoid experiments, and that some of them were too large, some too small, some of them were unable to work together... The Lemur is one such possibility. There may once have been lemur-like beings in actuality, about 500,000 years ago. They probably disappeared because they weren't aggressive enough. There's a theory developed by Robert Ardrey in a very interesting book called *African Genesis*, to the effect that man arose on the plains of Africa, and survived because he was a killer. "The aggressive southern ape" he calls him. "Not in Asia and not in innocence was man born. The home of our fathers was the African highlands on a sky-swept savanna glowing with menace."

Q : *Do you believe in the frequently reiterated promises of a future humanity made better by the development of automation, or technology in general?*

A : Decidedly not. It depends on who is directing the technology, technology being a more or less neutral instrument. We have seen nothing reassuring in that direction, with the present people in power, the more efficient the technology the more of a menace they are.

Q : Is there any escape from the "Nova Conspiracy"?

A : I think things are very much in the balance at the present time.

Q : In your books there are individuals classed in distinct categories—the factualists, the liquefactionists, the divisionists, for example. What do they represent?

A : This was in Naked Lunch and was rather a crude and tentative classification, and is I think explained there. It doesn't stand up too well at the present time and I wouldn't use the same categories.

Q : How does the extermination of resisters in the Nova Ovens take place right now?

A : The machine has many ways of dealing with anyone who is at all inconvenient. People like Wilhelm Reich, for example. Characterologically he was not set up to defend himself; he didn't have a sense of humor and he didn't realize who or what he was up against. They drove him first into paranoia, into mistakes, into ignoring federal injunctions and summonses. He was finally sent to jail and he died there. There are many other examples ... Drug laws are a pretext to extend police power, expand police personnel, and set up a police state with the aid of a controlled press. Drug laws are a pretext to smear anyone who opposes the police state. Front page: So-and-so in drug raid. Certain substances—sealing wax, cooking herbs, soap—were turned over to forensic laboratories for analysis. Two weeks later on the back page, no charges filed against so-and-so. Meanwhile, so-and-so has lost his job, been stripped and searched at seven airports, each search splashed across the front page. Never has the Mc-

Carthy principle of guilt by association been so shame-
fully applied as in the English press today.

Here are some quotes: "*Customs search two more pop
groups:* Two British pop groups' luggage and car were
searched by customs officers at Sidney Airport. The search
followed the seizure of two books from Eric Burdon:
Kenneth Anger's *The History of Eroticism* and *An Olympia Reader*, containing a selection of short stories by
Henry Miller and others." There are many ways in which
the press can inconvenience or incapacitate anyone who
gets in the way of the machine.

Q : What do you see as the cause of the desire for intellectual uniformity which seems to be so violently experienced by societies dominated by the power of money?

A : Intellectual uniformity is more and more necessary as
the contradictions and failures of the society become more
and more apparent. It has reached the point now where
it's practically a criminal offense to express a sensible
opinion. You express a moderate opinion about drugs,
and you're accused of advocating their use, and denounced as a criminal. Suggest that anything's basically
wrong with society, you're an anarchist striking at the very
roots of organized civilization. They cannot allow any
leeway because the contradictions are too blatant. Does
it exist in other sorts of societies as well? Well, of course.
It exists in both Russia and China to a marked degree.
It isn't only a question of money, it's a question of whatever the vested interest of power is. They cannot tolerate
any deviations from it.

Q : The Machine, we are promised, will save mankind in
the near future. How do you view this salvation?

A : Well, I don't see how it could possibly come about,
since the machine is directed by and must be operated by
someone, and it will depend on the intentions and intelligence of the operator. Wiener warned that the machine

can think a thousand times quicker than we can and that it may well sweep its masters to disaster before they know what the machine is about. You feed into the machine "Win the war in Vietnam at any cost," well, the machine goes ahead and does it, but you don't know what would happen. No, I don't see any salvation in the machine, in the machinery or technology or computing machines in the hands of the present individuals and groups in power on the planet.

Q : *Many consider censorship a useful safeguard, and think that not everyone should be exposed to everything. What do you think?*

A : I think that all censorship, any form of censorship, should be abolished. I don't think so-called dirty books ever inspired anyone to commit any crime more serious than masturbation. But there is a type of writing that does cause people to commit crimes, and that is writing done in the world press. Robert Benjamin Smith, 18, of Mesa, charged with the murder of four women and a young girl, November 12, in a Mesa beauty college, pleaded innocent Wednesday, by reason of insanity. Smith told Police Sergeant Ray Gomez he got the idea from mass killings in Chicago and in Austin, Texas.

Dig into your morgues and see how many times the prisoner got the idea from reading about it in the papers. The man that shot Rudy Dutschke got the idea from reading about Dr King.

The excuse for censorship of fiction, that it causes people to commit crimes, is absolutely ridiculous, in view of the crimes committed every day by people who got the idea from reading about it in the newspapers. And television is just about as bad, because in this medium you have news programs of things that are happening, and you also have fiction. Fiction in that juxtaposition seems to exert more of an influence: there are four or five recent cases of young people who hanged themselves after seeing a television Western. An additional factor is news programs on television, something actually happening, as opposed to fiction, which everyone knows is make-believe. People don't rush out and commit murders after reading Agatha Christie, but they certainly do commit murder after reading about other murders in the newspapers. Incidentally, all censorship, I understand, has just been removed in Denmark, with no effect whatever. In fact, statistics, uncertain as yet, indicate a decline in the incidence of rape, and sexual crimes of violence. What the people in control are trying to hide by censorship is the fact that if all censorship were removed, nothing would happen.

Q : In Boston, there was a trial over Naked Lunch. Norman Mailer and Allen Ginsberg testified for your defense. Were you present? What impression were you left with?

A : No, I was not. I was asked to be present but I refused. I was left with the impression that the whole thing was an absolute farce. The defense was trying to demonstrate that *Naked Lunch* has social significance, and this seems to me quite beside the point, and not really getting to the basic question of the right of censorship at all, the right of the government to exercise any censorship. I'm sure if I had been there I couldn't have done very much good.

Q : When people call a work pornographic, what do you think they mean?

A : I don't think it means a thing, and they don't either, because the definitions of what constitutes pornography, the legal definitions, are getting more and more confused. They say now if it has redeeming social significance, whatever that may be, it is not pornographic. And then, more and more contradictory judicial decisions—"Exploiting pornography for profit." Well, of course, any publisher expects to make a profit on his books. I think it's one of those double-barreled words with a derogatory connotation that has absolutely no precise meaning.

Q : *Do you think that pornography in the normal sense is present in things which pass the censors, but in disguised form?*

A : Oh, yes! They get away with an awful lot, undoubtedly; they slip an awful lot through. And, then of course, there's the whole question of the pornography of violence which is probably more likely to have a bad effect than sexual pornography, although I don't believe in any censorship at all, either in film, or on the stage, or in literature. Yes, certainly, they get away with an awful lot, just by keeping it a little bit under cover.

Q : *Is there a political path to the liberation of the world? Would a complete ideological change, the replacement of the capitalist world by a socialist world, for example, offer a solution?*

A : It would seem to me most emphatically no. Because these are just batting around the same old formulas. What happens, for example, when the government takes over the so-called means of production? Nothing. Our factories in the West are practically state-owned now. That is, a person may own a factory, but he is told how much he must pay his workers, how many people he can employ ... He's little more than a manager, and his position not much different than the manager of a Russian factory. I don't think it would make hardly any difference at all.

Q : *The anarchist is perhaps one of the few who offers a possible solution for the future. Do you believe in the solutions which he proposes?*

A : I don't really know what they are, although I would say this, that I don't believe in any solution that proposes halfway measures. Unless we can abolish the whole concept of the nation, and the whole concept of the family, we aren't going to get anywhere at all. It's the same thing with some other name. For example, I think there's no solution in the United Nations. United Nations—you've got it right built in there, *Nations*, that's the trouble. The anarchists say do away with all laws, but laws, of course, are a result of nations. It seems to me they don't go to the root of the difficulty, the basic formula, which is the formula of the nation, but rather they pose a solution for a *fait accompli* which isn't going to work. They leave the nation in existence, and say that we will abolish the laws. It's like trying to abolish the symptoms of a disease while leaving the disease itself untouched.

Q : Could the elimination of money alter the structures of society?

A : 1959, *Minutes To Go* I wrote: "I'm absolutely weak I can only just totter home darling the dollar has collapsed." *Minutes To Go* which incorporates the first cut-up experiments, has turned out to be a prophetic book. You see there is something wrong with the whole concept of money. It takes always more and more to buy less and less. Money is like junk. A dose that fixes you on Monday won't fix you on Friday. We are being swept with vertiginous speed into a worldwide inflation comparable to what happened in Germany after World War I. The rich are desperately stockpiling gold, diamonds, antiques, paintings, first editions, stamps, food, liquor, medicines, tools and weapons.

The scion of a well-known banking family once told me a family secret. When a certain stage of responsibility and awareness has been reached by a young banker he is taken to a room lined with family portraits in the middle of which is an ornate gilded toilet. Here he comes every day to defecate surrounded by the family portraits until he realizes that *money is shit*. And what does the money machine eat to shit it out? It eats youth, spontaneity, life,

beauty and above all it eats creativity. It eats quality and
shits out quantity. There was a time when the machine
ate in moderation from a plentiful larder and what it ate
was replaced. Now the machine is eating faster much
faster than what it eats can be replaced. That is why by
its nature money is worth always less. People want
money to buy what the machine eats to shit money out.
The more the machine eats the less remains. So your
money buys always less. This process is now escalating
geometrically. If the West does not start a nuclear war
first their monetary system will fall apart through the
inexorable consumption by the machine of life art flavor
beauty to make more and more shit which buys less and
less life art flavor beauty because there is less and less to
buy. The machine is eating it all. The time must come
when money will buy nothing because there will be nothing left for money to buy. Money will eliminate itself.

Q : *The Beat/Hip axis, notably in such figures as Ginsberg,
want to transform the world by love and nonviolence.
Do you share this interest?*

A : Most emphatically no. The people in power will not
disappear voluntarily, giving flowers to the cops just isn't
going to work. This thinking is fostered by the establishment; they like nothing better than love and nonviolence.
The only way I like to see cops given flowers is in a
flower pot from a high window.

Q : *Do you believe in the peace-bringing virtue of disarmament?*

A : No. It isn't going to occur, for one thing; it isn't occurring, can't occur, in terms of itself. As soon as you have
armaments, disarmament becomes very unlikely. The
whole absurdity of spending money on armaments in the
first place is an outgrowth of the basic formula of a nation; and until that formula is attacked at its vegetable
root, which is the biologic family, there isn't going to be

any real disarmament. . .just talk and committees and nonsense.

Q : *What do you think about capital punishment?*

A : A barbarous practice. Of course, it should be eliminated everywhere.

Q : *Do Good and Evil really exist?*

A : Not in the absolute sense. Something is good or evil according to your needs and the nature of your organism. What opposes or tries to annihilate any person or species is seen by that person or species as being evil. I think it's naive to predicate any absolutes there; it only has reference to the conditions of life of a given organism or species or society.

Q : *What do you think of the penal system?*

A : Preposterous, it's left over from the Middle Ages. In the first place, society makes all these criminals quite deliberately, these great concentration camps, where they dump people known as criminals. Many of them are psychopaths, that is, they are refractory to control. As soon as they become criminals, there will be no more trouble from them at all. They're right in that game of cops and robbers for life, in a concentration camp. But now they've begun extending this concentration camp, extending it and extending it, by making more laws and making more people criminals, if all the laws were enforced, they'd have practically everyone in the concentration camp, and everyone else would be necessary to guard them. They have reached an impasse: they must either admit that the whole thing is a farce and that laws are not meant to be enforced, or change them, or enforce them. And they're afraid to do any one of those three things. They cannot admit that the thing is a farce, they will not make any basic changes. Enforcing these laws would be, of course, the most dangerous thing they could do, in America they would have a good thirty to forty million people in jail; and how many would it take to arrest, guard, process these offenders? Well, you'd have the whole country a shell around a great sullen core of violators. How could they carry on with national defense if they put all the young people in jail? Where would their soldiers be in the event of an attack? They temporize, just the same way that England does. They won't make any basic changes. They keep saying it can't happen here; it happened in France, but England is different. The whole Western world is foundering in absolute stupidity, trying to make things work that can't possibly work.

Q : The Scandinavian countries are often cited as examples of successful countries.

A : It's an easy job; it's smaller. For example, in Denmark, they've got 4 million people, who are more or less homogeneous. They don't have a crime problem, you can't commit a crime in Denmark, everyone would know about it right away. They don't have any slums. They don't have any underworld, no place where people could dispose of stolen goods, they've really made crime, on any scale, impossible there. Of course, they have a very enlightened penal system for the people who do commit crimes, the occasional murder, same as in Sweden. They're simply smaller, more homogeneous countries and it's much easier to control the factors. There's no poverty there, you're not allowed to be poor. People are not very happy, but they're certainly well taken care of.

Q : Are they happy anywhere?

A : They're certainly happier in Spain with all the poverty than they are in Sweden with all the prosperity and their high living standard.

Q : But then, Spain is a good example of a highly controlled country with a repressive government, a religious bugbear—just about everything. . .

A : Just about everything. They have all sorts of troubles. But you see, poverty keeps people busy. You see happiness there in the faces of the people on the streets that you do not see on Swedish streets.

Q : "It is necessary always to create as many new conflicts as possible, and always aggravate existing conflicts." Could that be a definition of politics?

A : Yes, I think someone has written a book recently pointing out that war is absolutely essential to the maintenance of modern society, and they've always got to keep one going somewhere. They're necessary both psychologically and economically. You see, the whole concept of a nation depends on the hostility of another nation on the other side of a line. If you didn't have that factor of hostility, if there were no conflicts of interest and politicians couldn't create any conflicts, the lines would break down. And they wouldn't have a nation to rule.

Q : What would happen in a state in which "normal" men ruled?

A : Well, I object to the word normal; I don't know what it means.

Q : Average people who might be intolerant of, might suffocate extraordinary people.

A : I think it would be an absolute nightmare, and it's very likely to occur, because with overpopulation there are more and more so-called normal men, that is, just ordinary stupid sons of bitches. That's another great problem, this overpopulation, which results from the concept of a nation, the necessity for armies, and the necessity for large numbers of people to produce and consume

consumer goods. With overpopulation the quality of the
human stock is declining disastrously. They're becoming
more and more stupid, more and more incompetent, and
there are more and more of them.

Q : What do you think of contemporary America?

A : At the official level a nightmare. Difficult to believe
that people in positions of power who form the foreign
and domestic policies of America could be so stupid and
so basically ill-intentioned. Conformity on the part of a
vast middle class—(the Wallace folks)—and dissent on
the part of young people, intellectuals and the professions have reached an unprecedented scale. I don't think
there is any country where dissent is so widespread or
where dissent has a better chance of effecting basic
changes. I think more is happening in America today in
the sphere of politics and the arts than is happening anywhere else. Censorship has almost ceased to exist. Of
course any visitor from the old world—and returning
after so many years in Europe and Africa I have the eyes
of a visitor—is impressed by the standard of comfort and
service. Central heating. Good inexpensive food right by
your door at any hour of the day or night. I say without
reservations America now has the best food in the world
and for the money you spend it is perhaps the cheapest
country in the world. Certainly much cheaper than London, Rome or Paris. I have just returned from America
and found that it has changed almost beyond recognition since I was last there three years ago. America may
well be the hope of the world. It is also the source of
such emotional plagues as drug hysteria, racism, Bible
belt morality, Protestant capitalistic ethic, muscular
Christianity that have spread everywhere transforming this
planet into an annex of Hell.

Q : Do you conceive a way in which the U.S.A. can sur-
mount the problems posed by foreign policy and integra-
tion without undergoing a radical governmental change?

A : No, I do not. There's not a politician in America that will admit that there's anything basically wrong. They think you can just patch the thing together and they will not examine their basic premises and realize that the whole thing is unworkable. It can't possibly work. And naturally, if they just patch things together, which is all they're very likely to do, things are going to get worse and worse and worse. And I think the most likely change would be some form of extreme rightist fascism, a take-over by the army. Very likely to occur. Contrary to what Marx believed, of course, industrialized countries go fascist, and it's the unindustrialized countries that go communist. You might get communism in South America, but it's very unlikely that you'll get it in America at the present time.

Q : Does the question of Vietnam seem to you a characteristic problem which the U.S.A. will encounter again and again?

A : Obviously, they will encounter it again and again. First was Korea, now it's Vietnam. If they ever settle that, it'll be some place else. This whole idea of containing communism on a global scale can only result in commitment to one such nonsensical venture after the other. Certainly it will happen again somewhere else, it's bound to. Any rightist government has only to say they're fighting communism and involve the Americans.

Q : What is your stand on Vietnam?

A : I don't as a rule interfere in political matters. Once a problem has reached the political-military stage, it is already insoluble. However, I sometimes think out loud: the French were in Indo-China, if my memory serves, quite some years before they found out they were losing at any exchange rate of casualties...losing their professional soldiers; and they found out again in Algeria. Now, you take a formula like Nationalism-Army Police-Trouble

with other stone-age tribes...and when they start using
atomic bombs instead of stone axes—closing time, gentle-
men... Well, looks like some folks figure the only solution to this mess is to blow up the set and start over.
Many have happened several times already, the species
being about five hundred years old, and what we call
history dating back only ten thousand years—give a little,
take a little. What were they doing for four hundred and
ninety thousand years? We have come from stone axes
to nuclear weapons in ten thousand years. This may have
happened several times before. It all does seem rather
familiar like where we came in.

Now, if you don't want to see the whole set go up, of
course the Americans should get out of Vietnam before
..."American and Chinese troops clash north of Hanoi";
..."Johnson in the toughest speech yet";..."Kosygin
bluntly warned"... And, of course, every nation should
destroy their atomic weapons and maybe their atomic
physicists as well, to make sure. But even that would
pose quite a disposal problem, and is, if I may add, extremely unlikely to occur. Weapons are made to be used,
and used they will be, sooner or later, so long as the
formula can never be dissolved in terms of itself. That is,
in political-military terms.

Q : Is the destruction of the police machine still possible?

A : Possibly, yes. The machine is certainly on the defensive
at the present time, and with enough resistance, worldwide, it is still possible. Of course, the police machine
isn't going to be smashed until we destroy with it the
whole concept of a nation. I see a future where guerrilla
armies of liberation have arisen in South and Central
America and Africa. "We will march on the police machine. Everywhere, we will destroy it. We will destroy
the machine and all its records, and we will destroy the
house organ of the police machine which goes under the
name of conservative press."

Q : Uranium Willy tries to give life to mankind: "Prisoners
of the Earth, come out!," he cries. Are there still enough
Uranians on earth to tear down the walls of prisons?

A : Well, they seem to be doing a pretty good job of it
lately: France, Stockholm, Germany, America ... Pretty
worldwide. It would seem that the message of total resistance is indeed out on the short wave of the world.

Q : What is your stand on student rioting and violence?

A : There should be more riots and more violence. Young
people in the West have been lied to, sold out, and be-
trayed. Best thing they can do is take the place apart
before they are destroyed in a nuclear war. Nuclear war
is inevitable if the present controllers remain in power.
   Young people pose the only effective challenge to
established authority. Established authority is well aware
of the challenge. Established authority is moving against
young people everywhere. It is now virtually a crime to
be young. This is all-out war in which the opposition
will use the dirtiest tactics at their disposal. The only
country to gain the support of its young people is Red
China, and that is why the State Department has put a
travel ban on Red China. They don't want Americans
to see and realize that any country which offers young
people anything at all will gain their support. The Western establishments offer nothing. They have nothing to
declare but their bad intentions. Well, let them come
all the way out in the open with their bad intentions.
If it comes to that, any number can play. The student
rebellion is now a worldwide movement. Never before in
recorded history has established authority been so basically
challenged on a worldwide scale. However, the incidents
that trigger student uprisings are often insignificant: the
dismissal of a liberal professor, a refusal to change the
examination system or to meet other demands for minor
changes. A crucial reason for all young people to rebel

is the issue of top secret research carried on in universities or anywhere else. *All knowledge all discoveries belong to everybody.* Top secret classified research means research opposed to the interests of youth, knowledge withheld from youth, discoveries used against youth. *A worldwide monopoly of knowledge and discoveries for counter-revolutionary purposes is the basic issue.* Betrayal and deceit is involved here far beyond the traditional conservative reluctance to meet the demands for increased freedom on the part of young people. *All knowledge all discoveries belong to you by right. It is time to demand what belongs to you.* To put it country simple the game is rigged. Who is the aggressor in a three-card monte game like this the "rube" who finds out he has been cheated and tries to get his money back or the crooked dealers?

I quote from recent article in *Mayfair* magazine, entitled "The Fire Breaks Out":*

The uneasy spring of 1969. Under the pretext of drug control, suppressive police states have been set up throughout the Western world. The precise programming of thought, feeling, and apparent sensory impressions by the technology outlined in Bulletin 2332 enables the police states to maintain a democratic façade from behind which they loudly denounce as criminals, perverts, and drug addicts, anyone who opposes the control machine. Underground armies operate in the big cities, enturbulating the police with false information through anonymous phone calls and letters. Police, with drawn guns, erupt at the senator's dinner party. . .a very special dinner party too, that would tie up a sweet thing in surplus planes. "We've been tipped off a nude reefer party is going on here. Take the place apart, boys; and you folks keep your clothes on, or I'll blow your filthy guts out!" We put out false alarms on the police short wave, directing patrol cars to nonexistent crimes and riots, which enables us to strike somewhere else. Squads of false police search and beat the citizenry. False construction workers tear up streets,

* Published in a slightly altered form in *Evergreen Review*, No. 67; June, 1969, as "My Mother and I Would Like to Know."

rupture water mains, cut power connections. Infrasound
machines set off every burglar alarm in the city. Our aim is
total chaos.

In Mexico, South and Central America, guerrilla units are
forming an army of liberation to free the United States. In
Africa, corresponding units, from Tangier to Timbuktu, prepare to liberate Western Europe and the United Kingdom.
Despite disparate aims and personnel of its constituent members, the underground is agreed on basic objectives. . . We
intend to march on the police everywhere. We intend to
destroy the police machine and all its records. We intend to
destroy the house organ of the world police machine, that
goes under the name of conservative press. We intend to
destroy all dogmatic verbal systems. The family unit and its
cancerous expansion into tribes, countries, nations, we will
eradicate at the vegetable root. We don't want to hear any
more family talk, mother talk, father talk, cop talk, priest talk,
country talk or party talk. To put it country simple, we have
heard enough bullshit!

Q : *Any comments on the assassination of Robert Ken-
nedy?*

A : It seems likely that the assassination was arranged by
the far right, and that the arrangers are now taking this
opportunity to pass anti-gun laws, and disarm the nation
for the fascist takeover. That will certainly occur, if
America is involved in a war with China. As to how such
assassinations are arranged, there are very definite techniques for doing this. Assassins often hear voices telling
them to kill. Are these voices necessarily imaginary?
Directional mikes can project voices. Top secret research
on lasers is concerned with sending thoughts. Experiments
in Norway indicate the possibility of activating word patterns in the brain by tape-recorder techniques. The following story explores these possibilities. . .

23 SKIDOO

I work for the 23 Screwball Department. We got our
files on all nut cases and each case is classified like 23:

could write a threatening letter or slither an unloaded
blank cartridge pistol at a queen if we nerved him up to
it definitely not 23. . . :::that is assassin timber now for
that the old reliable is the quiet type read the Bible kept
to himself faraway look in his eyes it was a dreamy look
and at the same time it was a disagreeable look but nobody liked to look at it so it passed unnoticed until one
day just as the Consul got out of his car at 10:23 A.M. he
was amazed to be approached by what he took to be an
uncouth beggar carrying a Bible in one hand and in the
other what later turned out when extracted from the
Consul's spine after repeatedly penetrating his liver and
abdomen to be an eight-inch boning knife. As he struck
the assassin was heard to say: "After all God made
knives."

Overpowered by consular guards and turned over to the
police the assassin admitted to being a member of the
dreaded "Fly Tox Movement" an extremist sect who hold
hashish in horror getting their kicks largely from vitamin
deficiency a preparation like that you can get on his line
sweet and clear "Can you hear me Homer? Of course you
can. I'm telling you what you have to do Homer. We will
protect you Homer. Flying saucers will be waiting after
you have done our bidding."

Now it sometimes happens you lose a screwball can't
get on his line well then you put everybody with cop in
him out on the streets to trace down the lost screwball
before he talks too sensible about what we are doing here
in this department which is unthinkable because we got
here first heavy and cold as a cop's blackjack on a winter
night we was looking for a lost screwball last contacted
in an orgone accumulator screen went dead case like that
usually turns out to be interdepartmental sabotage or
illegal recruitment the whole department is rotten with
it maybe the Ethnology Department used him in a ritual
murder we are men of the world these things happen. . .

"Joe may my flesh rot if this department knows what

you are talking about." Right through the departments
cold hate of a questioned accountant who knows his
books are right. We had to face the possibility our ball
had been nutnipped and might be used to exterminate
one of our own white-haired boys like the Old Sugar
Boss. At the office party Mr Blankslip from accounting
mixed his "blackout special" and a little cold voice told
him this man must be killed to save the Lamb of God
from the Beast 666 as a member of the special squadron
your duty is clear comrade a man has his simple job to do
for Total Oil the company always takes care of its own
you didn't think I'd let you down son? God? Well not
exactly just a plain Joe with a job to do like you've got a
job to do now faced by the unspeakable Old Sugar Boss
after three Martinis letting his co-workers he calls us know
we are all jolly decent plain Joes like him he had a slimy
way say if a member of the staff came into the office without his shoes shined the boss would stop having his own
shoes shined and call attention to it at all times receiving
a foreign dignitary apologized for the state of his shoes "as
a matter of office procedure you understand" until you
got the hint and came in with your shoes like obsidian
mirrors and the boss smiles slow like stiff molasses and
says "Good to see you" or he would leave a small sum of
money out on the desk then pinch it himself most likely.

"Oh uh Grimsy?"

"Yes sir."

"You didn't happen to see fifteen shillings on my desk
did you? Thought you might have put it in petty cash?
No? lying right there on the desk. . ."

"I didn't see it sir."

"Well it's not important. . . Good night Grimsy. . ."

"Good night sir."

"Oh. . .Grimsy. . ."

"Yes sir."

"If you need an advance on your salary you can ask
for it you know. . ."

He had a way of dropping in on his staff at any time
no staff member was permitted to have locks on his doors
not even the bathroom any hour of the day or night the
Old Sugar Boss throws your door open and smiles at you.

"Well writing late in our diary? That must make interesting reading."

Clearly O.I.—Outside Influence—is at work. Whole
sections of the machine are now riddled and clogged by
what the Party Chairman termed "God-eyed Communist
buffoons who are sabotaging important projects."

We must trace down all cases of lost contact though
like I say most of them turn out to be interdepartmental
louseups you get in a creep outfit like this but you never
know when a lost ball has fallen under O.I. until the
damage is done. When you see their ball my friend it is
too late.

"Get your hands off me you filthy old bum."

just so happens empty street doorman around the
corner for a "rouge"...bleeding profusely he was carried
into the lobby where he described his assailant as "wearing a light blue suit stained down the front with scrambled eggs and smelling abominably of raw onions and
cheap spirits."

The attacker had disappeared.

"To be used again in some other garb of course."

My superior nodded "Some old nut with pamphlets.
You attempt to brush by him..."

O.I. could screw up our whole department since we
have now perfected and demonstrated in the field operation Mass 23 Skiddoo...:::Indonesia:::....induced by
computerized techniques in otherwise normal population
a leak at this stage is simply unthinkable it could unthink
the whole department preoccupied with these thoughts
he was amazed to be stopped rather roughly by a gendarme.

"See here I'm from the Ministry of Interior." He

glanced sharply at the agent "Why that uniform is a fake."

He looked around for a proper cop and died without regaining consciousness. The assassin, described by police as "the professional brother of a cop" said the Under Secretary made a threatening gesture and he fired in self-defense. Day like another quiet American eating scrambled eggs in Nedicks suddenly the Filipino cook came from behind the counter moving with a strangely purposeful trot...

"New man on the job...eager to please" the quiet American thought. He smiled warmly "Warm my eggs up will you Jojo?"

cold eggs cold coffee cold American on the floor.

"Hello señor you like my country yes?"

"Why sure Mother and me both love Mexico. Won't you join us in a beer?"

"Two gringos more or less between machos I was crude."

Her first thought was she must have left something in the restaurant and this horrid young man in a black leather jacket was running out to give it to her she was much too rich to tip him but what was that in his hand exactly? The grenade blew her mink coat fifty yards.

Man he thought was a new doorman barring his way to the Yale Club suddenly produced a bottle doused him with gasoline and set him on fire.

You never know when damage is done for that old reliable is late and an orgone accumulator screen went dead on a winter night like that usually turns out screen went dead and the whole department is illegal Mr Blankslip mixed his black out Lamb of God from the Beast 666 now faced by the unspeakable Ethnology Department all his co-workers he calls us know these things happen by Joes like him he had a slimy way say of talking right through my flesh Old Sugar Boss after three Martinis.

"We are all jolly decent plain Joes slob clear."

grenade. . .anteroom of the consulate a new doorman barring his way light blue suit stained down the front doused with gasoline I was crudo a gendarme.

"Won't you have a beer?"

Regaining consciousness assassins stalk the passer-by and all brothers of a cop said Swedish Consul quietly eating scrambled eggs in Nedicks. . .

Oswalds and Rubys were but plates dropped from out pockets human time bombs exploded on computerized order. Now all precision is lost. Random assassins and buffoons prowl the street and all this anarchy resulted from one lost ball.

And who do you think was the first agent on the golf course? Quite by chance the same stranger here? After all I am 23. . .:::

Q : *Doesn't man prefer his prison to the discovery of a new space?*

A : I don't think so. I think only the man that has been so absolutely beaten down and conditioned by the machine that he doesn't have any thoughts of his own feels that way. Of course, that's what's going to happen to most people because, statistically, most people will believe what they're told and will be overwhelmed by their conditions. However, they aren't getting enough percentage of submission now to prevent very serious resistance. Their position has never been more seriously threatened than it is in the present moment.

Q : *The torture of the "Switchboard" which you describe in Naked Lunch—is it the normal process for reaching "civilization?"*

A : It's the normal process of conditioning people to believe what they're told.

Q : *You frequently speak in your books about "becoming oneself." What is implied in this search for oneself?*

A : Well, I think what is implied is a self that one is, apart from imposed thinking.

DON'T HAVE TO THINK

I have just come back from a walk in the garden. It is 6 o'clock and everyone in my section is taking showers. I pass several young men in shorts and bathrobes carrying towels. I don't perspire much. I sit down in my room and open the window and light a cigarette. On the floor of my room the two servants who cook and serve the food are giving their little girl a geography lesson maps spread out on the floor. I watch them through cigarette smoke. Their presence does not touch me. The center is somewhere in Austria and at this time in midsummer it is hot and sticky. I have been here about a month. What I am here to learn is a new way of thinking. There are no lessons and no teachers. There are no books and no work to be done. I do almost nothing. The first step is to stop doing everything you "have to do." Mock up a way of thinking you have to do. This is one exercise derived from Scientology we have all studied at one time or another. Exercise loosens the hold of enforced thinking and extends the range of don't have to think.

Example: You have to run the things you are going to do today write letters call so-and-so take clothes to laundry see about getting the radiators fixed. You run these items ten times when once is already too much. So mock up a run of imaginary errands. Now mock up some thinking you don't have to do. Select a person whose way of life is completely different from yours and mock up his thinking.

(Example: You have to mock up interviews or situations in which you play an effective role before imaginary audience. Well, mock some up. Now mock up some enforced thinking you don't have to do, somebody else's enforced thinking what Dutch Schultz the numbers racketeer had to think, what a hotel manager has to think what a poor Moroccan farmer has to think.)

Wind up is you don't have to think anything. And
then? In this section there are students like myself. I
share my room with one of them. He is taking a shower.
It is a long narrow room like a corridor high ceiling
stained marble fireplace toilet articles on the shelf above
it two narrow beds two wardrobes a porcelain stove disconnected
for the summer. There is a potted rubber
plant on top of the stove. I am sitting in a worn leather
armchair by the window which has panes of some plastic
like they use to cover the greenhouse and seed beds in
the garden. There is a sink with a mirror on a nail for
washing and shaving. The door is open on a portico and
beyond is a garden where we eat under vine trellises.
Dinner will be at seven a fruit soup, meat, salad, beer, a
pudding or dumpling. After dinner I will walk in the
château garden down by the fish pools and throw bread to
the fish or sit in the common room which has leather sofas
and bronze statues old copies of the *Illustrated London
News* picture periodicals in German and Italian. I can't
say much about the roommate. He is a vague shape under
a thin blanket. Mostly we don't see each other since he
is out of the room when I am here. I do know he is a
student like me and not a staff member. The staff members
are distinguished from students by the fact that they
have duties however light. They are couriers expediters
and the like that is they sometimes deliver messages or
carry boxes from one place to another. The staff members
resent the students and greet us with eyes averted muttering
sullenly. There is only one person I have seen that
gives orders to the staff. This is a young woman who lives
in the château above the garden. She occasionally comes
out to send some staff member to find another or to give
instructions to the gardener. He complained to me this
afternoon that "she expects me to get down in the ground
and grow there myself." The grounds are not well maintained
and the general impression is one of neglect. The
cooking for our section is done by a fat middle-aged
woman. Her husband serves the meals and does just
enough cleaning so our quarters are bearable. He wears

lederhosen and smokes a clay pipe. Coffee and rolls in the morning, cold soup fish and fruit for lunch, soup, and dessert for dinner. Beer is served only with dinner. At lunch we have cider.

The new way of thinking has nothing to do with logical thought. It is no oceanic organismal subconscious body thinking. It is precisely delineated by what it is not. Not knowing what is and is not knowing we know not. Like a moving film the flow of thought seems to be continuous while actually the thoughts flow stop change and flow again. At the point where one flow stops there is a split-second hiatus. The new way of thinking grows in this hiatus between thoughts. I am watching the servants on the floor pointing to the map and not thinking anything about what I see at all. My mind moves in a series of blank factual stops without labels and without questions. The objects around me the bodies and minds of others are just there and I move between them without effort or comment. There is nothing to do here, no letters to answer no bills to pay no goals barriers or penalties. There are no considerations here that would force thinking into certain lines of structural or environmental necessities. The new way of thinking is the thinking you would do if you didn't have to think about any of the things you ordinarily think about if you had no work to do nothing to be afraid of no plans to make. Any exercises to achieve this must themselves be set aside. It's a way you would think if you didn't have to think up a way of thinking you don't have to do. We learn to stop words to see and touch words to move and use words like objects.

The servants have gone to fix dinner. I kick off my slippers and stand up. I take off my shirt slip off pants and underwear and sit down naked in the chair feeling the leather where the late afternoon breeze has touched it cool against my back. All of us have had more or less the same training. I see a red brick building over a river dim jerky far away: the Academy. The original academy program was predicated on the assumption that such an academy could be established without opposition. The assumption proved erroneous. Never have the forces of suppression been more desperately mobilized to block any training that would enable students to challenge the parasitic persistence of unworkable establishments. In consequence academy training had to be decentralized and camouflaged. We take karate and Aikido training in the schools scattered through large cities of the world, our Scientology training at Scientology centers. Other courses are provided by a network of institutes and foundations often short-lived. The training is often interrupted. Three months of karate then Scientology take up all my time and just before the advanced Scientology courses I am shifted to Cairo for an intensive course in Egyptian hieroglyphs. This center is closed down by the government. After that there is a weapons course financed by a rightist billionaire in East Texas where we learn to use every weapon from a crossbow to a laser gun, a seminar in black magic of Africa sponsored by an ethnology institute in London that is always short of funds, a volunteer experiment in prolonged sense withdrawal set up by the U.S. Navy which ended in a Congressional investigation of brainwashing, a free fall club in North Dakota, skin diving and just when I am getting used to the aqualung we are thrown out of Ceylon where the program is and I do a Yoga stint in Northern India. Next thing I was exposed to DOR in Norway. The reference book on DOR is Wilhelm Reich's *Selected Writings* published by the Noonday Press of New York page 351 Orgone Physics. In its simplest form Reich's orgone accumulator is a box of wood or any organic material lined with sheet iron. More powerful accumulators can be made by adding additional layers of iron and organic material and accumulators of 100 alternate layers have been constructed.

In 1950 Reich discovered that even small quantities of radioactive material placed in an orgone accumulator give rise to what he calls DOR—Deadly Orgone Radiation. Exposure to DOR can produce severe symptoms or death, but gradual exposure to controlled dosage builds up a generalized immunity. I quote from "Orgone Physics":

"The experiments were planned with the prospect of finding a powerful antidote against nuclear radiation sickness." The experiments turned out to be more dangerous than he had anticipated. Workers experienced the following symptoms: a penetrating salty taste turning slightly bitter or sour on the outstretched tongue, severe conjunctivitis, nausea, a springlike pressure around the forehead, cold shivers alternating with hot flashes. In some cases the skin became mottled. In addition to these general symptoms DOR "attacked each person at his or her weakest point." Those who had a history of liver illness became jaundiced etcetera. However, the effect of DOR was to bring the illness into the open and eliminate it. "Not only did all workers return to good health after a few weeks more they felt particularly strong and active after DOR was disrupted. We have the distinct impression that those who had participated in the experiments had developed a certain immunity to the DOR effects. We have obtained a most powerful weapon against radiation sickness. However the health qualities of DOR will be obtainable only by careful dosage." One doctor working on this project nearly died as a result of overexposure to DOR.

February 19, 1951: 12:30 P.M.

Protocol on....................M.D.

"I put my head inside the accumulator for a moment and felt suddenly as if hit with a sledge hammer on my head. I began to feel fear which increased until it was the most severe death anxiety that I have ever experienced. I was semi-conscious, dizzy, could not see clearly. My pulse was very weak and slow, between 45 and 48. I had a hard time breathing. I felt as if I were going to die just simply stop.

"A criminal hater of mankind or a political enemy could easily drop activated DOR devices looking like simple metal lined boxes. . . There is no possibility of protecting oneself against DOR. It penetrates everything and cannot be shielded off by any amount of lead bricks aprons or masks. The scope of DOR energy in intensity as well as extensity is to the scope of atomic energy as is

infinity to a grain of sand". . . Remember that even a
wrist watch with radium dial taken into an accumulator
can produce marked symptoms of DOR. Reich was ex-
perimenting with very small quantities of radium. Clearly
a pile of fissionable material placed in a 1000-layer accumulator could produce unimaginable disaster.

"On the other hand, by gradual exposure, perhaps a
mass immunization to radiation sickness could be carried
out."

The center is all glass and steel shining in the cold
northern sunlight. Just to look at it I could see mad
scientists with wild blue eyes toasting each other in liquid
air as they release the last weapon from a polar installa-
tion. The director looks like Hammarskjöld's ghost. He
has the deadest voice I ever heard.

"The uh suppression of Doctor Reich's experiments and
the removal of his books from circulation underlines a
probability that the uh authorities in question intend to
use DOR against any uh dissident elements. You will
readily appreciate the uh advisability of acquiring the
corresponding immunity". . . He pressed a buzzer.

"Doctor Anderson will expose you."

Doctor Anderson looks at me and says "Hello there
young guy." He leads the way down a long white corridor
to a sunny room with a glass wall facing the inevitable
fjord. There is a couch by the window and a table of light
wood on which water hyacinths are growing in a yellow
bowl. The room smells of ozone and flowers. Doctor
Anderson motions me to a chair opposite what looks like
a bust wrapped in bandages.

"We call her Medusa, now isn't that cute?" He fiddles
with some dials above Medusa's head and steps to one
side. Something slides off Medusa's right shoulder and
hits me right in the heart. I am dying. Heart breathing
brain stops. I try to tell him I am dying without a throat
without a tongue. I come to on the couch the doctor
checking my pulse. He puts his hands on his hips and
looks down at me.

"Well chicken I think you'll live."

I sit up and then stand up.

"How do you feel?"

"High, man, floating."

I look out the glass wall and that post card fjord explodes in my brain green and pink and blue.

"You'll be wanting a sauna now."

I get nine exposures over a three-week period. By the end of the series I hardly feel it at all. The director tells me I am now immune.

"It is too early to say precisely how far-reaching the effects are. . .evidence as yet inconclusive would tend to suggest that the aging process is arrested or in any case retarded by gradient exposure to DOR. I will tell you in strictest confidence that you may be in a sense immune to death itself."

And I said: "What would believe it?"

There are study courses in virology, linguistics and general semantics, a course in assassination techniques, an improvised weapons and riot course. Any one of these disciplines could become a way of life but there is someone we never see who keeps us moving and rotating. The point is to apply what we have learned from one discipline to another and not get stuck in one way of doing things. Sometimes I am together with other academy students in a course but more often I am not. I have never seen any of these students before. They all had the academy look at once probing and impersonal remote and alert. I can tell what training the others have had a Scientology thank you, Aikido one point, a way of dressing from the hieroglyph course, a way of looking at fire extinguishers, kitchen knives and bicycle pumps form the improvised weapons course—(Remember the homemade lasers that sprayed out at the sides, infrasound whistles setting off burglar alarms for miles around, projector and DOR guns, a signal switch screen that alternated friendly and snarling faces 24 times per second, catapults and blowguns, devices for producing coal dust and sawdust explosions.)

My roommate comes in at this point with a towel

around his hips. I have never seen him before. I know that his name is Harper. His body is a mold filled with light, a mold that will soon be empty. I think this is the last course. The courses are all toys in a game of survival. The hunter must hunt to live. Saber-toothed tigers threaten the hunter. Look at factories and atom bombs. Artifacts, toys in a game of survival. Nations must produce to live. The Chinese and the Russians threaten our peaceful cities. Look at the human brain. This too is an artifact. "The St. Louis Academy was a rambling red brick building on a bluff over the river. A twilight like blue dust was settling into the river valley when Bill Harper a beginning student descended from a horse-drawn carriage cool remote Sunday fresh southerly winds a long time ago."

Light years away the academy that never was and never could have been. The Brain could not let it happen or it would have happened thousands of years ago. The Brain will not allow you to find out how easy it is to solve problems. Once problems are solved the brain artifact becomes obsolete. What is a problem? Mr Hubbard has defined a problem as postulate counter postulate, intention counter intention. The brain artifact has a built-in mechanism that prevents it from solving problems and that mechanism is The Word. The Brain can only produce more survival artifacts that produce more problems. In this last course we have rubbed out the word. The brain artifact with its self-limiting word mechanism is now obsolete. It is not made of metal or flint. It will leave no trace behind except the limestone mold of an empty house.

Q : You wrote: "I am not two, I am one." What are the consequences of this unity?

A : I've spoken of unworkable formulas and possibly the most unworkable formula is the whole concept of a dualistic universe. I don't think that there is really room for more than one person, that is, one will, on any planet. As soon as you get two you get trouble. Dualism is the whole basis of this planet—good and evil, communism, fascism, man, woman, etc. As soon as you have a formula like that, of course you're going to have trouble. The planet is populated by various groups and their conditions of life are completely incompatible and they aren't going to get together. It isn't a question of their just getting together and loving each other: they can't, 'cause their interests are not the same. Just take men and women for example, they'll never get together, their interests are not the same.

Q : What is the value of intelligence in the search for one-self?

A : Intelligence I would define simply as the ability to adapt oneself to new situations and environments and solve problems, obviously a useful instrument that will probably be laid aside eventually. The whole human brain is actually an artifact and when you don't need an artifact, you throw it away.

Q : The value of science?

A : Science? I don't know how you'd define science. We know in general what we mean by it: an overall method of evaluating information according to experimental data, and as such it is obviously valuable.

Q : "Nothing Is True—Everything Is Permitted," Hassan i Sabbah says. Is this the principle of freedom?

A : Yes, I would say that. If nothing is true, then everything is permitted. That is, if we realize that everything is illusion, then any illusion is permitted. As soon as we say that something is true, real, then immediately things are not permitted.

Q : Is love a solution?

A : I don't think so at all. I think love is a virus. I think love is a con put down by the female sex. I don't think that it's a solution to anything.

Q : *How do you feel about human beings?*

A : They have possibilities of development, but they aren't
going to realize them unless they can get rid of the
factors and the individuals who are suppressing them and
deliberately keeping them right where they are, not only
suppressing them but shoving them down further so
they're getting stupider and stupider. Nothing basically
wrong with the human beings themselves, but they certainly will have to take a very basic forward step in evolution. It's quite probable that at the real beginning point
of what we call modern man was speech. In the beginning
was the word. I think the next step will have to be beyond the word. The word is now an outmoded artifact.
Any life form that gets stuck with an outmoded built-in
artifact is doomed to destruction. The dinosaurs survived
because they were large and then they got larger and
larger and this ultimately of course led to their extinction.
The present form of human being quite possibly results
from words, and unless they get rid of this outmoded
artifact, it will lead to their extinction.

Q : *You speak of the necessity of breaking down the whole
formula of separate countries and nations. How can this
be brought about?*

A : At the present time we all are confined in concentration
camps called nations. We are forced to obey laws to which
we have not consented, and to pay exorbitant taxes to
maintain the prisons in which we are confined. The pretext that there is any measure of consent involved or
benefits received is wearing very thin indeed. The American people did not even know the atom bomb existed.
Still less were they consulted as to whether or not it
should be used. Thus, one of the most disastrous decisions
in human history was made by a few incompetent, ill-
informed, and ill-intentioned men. How can the concept
of the nation be attacked?

1. By the withdrawal of like-minded individuals into separate communities within nations. The Black Muslims are

moving in that direction. So are the Hippies. Other pref-
erential units could be set up: all male communities, ESP
communities, health communities, karate and judo communities, glider balloonist communities, yoga communities, Reichian communities, silence and sense-withdrawal
communities. Such communities would soon become international and break down national borders. It is an appli-
cation of the principles set forth in the academy series.

2. In 1961, Herr Doktor Kurt Unruh von Steinplatz enunciated his theory of authority units or simultaneous
governments. The authority unit is a set, simple or elaborate, that gives the apparency of authority. The apparency
of authority *is* authority. The simplest form would be a
police box that can be set up in growth areas to extort
money from tourists. Fade out to misty night in Mexico.
Three young men have pooled their resources and bought
an Unruh Box. They lounge about trying to give the shed
a lived-in look. Car should be along any minute now.

"Ah here is our first client."

Chain across the road flashlight in the face.

"Get out señores. Passport control."

Two American tourists on their way to Acapulco. The
cab driver comes along as interpreter.

"He say something wrong your passport. Passport muy
malo. You pay fine one hundred Mexican dollars."

"Why that's ridiculous. Tell him I won't pay a cent."

"He say no pay you go six months in the jail."

Right by the police box is a courtyard with heavy iron
grid and padlock. Inside are all the cripples lepers half-wits
and lunatics of the village assembled by an offer of free
food and pulque.

"Hello Johnny we fuck you inside."

"I want the American consul."

"Good evening Rodriguez. I happened to be passing
by."

"Here your consul Meester."

The consul peers at him nearsightedly. "Now we in the
State Department don't give advice to American citizens
but we sometimes think out loud. We know Americans

are being victimized but we can't do one thing about it.
If you raise a stink at this level it goes to a higher authority and that means more money. Meanwhile you are inside there and it might be months before we could get
you out. One poor fellow lost his mind in there. Off the
record it's cheaper to pay up. . . Oh uh excuse me." There
is a consultation outside the police box while one cop
watches the tourists fingering his gun butt as he hums
"La Cucaracha." The consul comes back in.

"This is more serious than I thought. Seems the driver
had cocaine in the car. Said you told him to put it there.
You could get ten years under Mexican law. Meanwhile
you are inside maybe two years before the case comes to
trial." The consul looks at the tourists. "How much can
you boys raise. . . Six hundred dollars in traveler's checks?
I don't know it might work. Just sign these checks."

Operating from a shed in Casablanca, the Herr Doktor
began turning out his prefabricated police boxes, complete
with three uniforms, guns, and official forms. He went on
to develop more elaborate units. Renting anonymous
buildings in large cities, he set up jails and courts. The
target is arrested by detectives, taken to jail (where he is
allowed to see his counsel and to consult an attorney),
tried, fined, imprisoned or even executed. For five million
dollars he can deliver a small country complete with army,
police and customs. For 23 billion, a deluxe unit with an
old style atom bomb and space program. These authority
units honeycombed the Western world, destroying the
whole concept of authority, as an unlimited flood of undetectable counterfeit money would destroy the monetary
system.

(It must be noted in passing that the good doctor was
not in all respects a tactful man. When asked by the
editor of a woman's magazine what he thought about the
"woman question" he replied jovially:

"Vy not cut off the head? Chickens can live so without
the head nourished from tubers it is of course the same
with womans. So brought to her true purpose of bearing
strong male children she finds her simple contentment is

it not? I appeal to you as a woman of good will to facili-
tate my experiments.")

In his four-volume treatise on the nature, development
and terminal stages of the Authority Virus he predicts
that the American Moral Disease will cripple the West
intellectually, artistically and technically by a systematic
persecution of anyone who rises above an average human
level of performance. This persecution will first be directed against entertainers and artists as the population
segment most refractory to control, but will soon extend
to scientists and technicians. The rich will be stripped of
their money by the very officials they have appointed to
protect privileged positions. He predicts that vast guerrilla armies will arise in South America and in Africa; that
these armies will attract the young of America and Europe,
that fugitive millionaires will finance the guerrillas, that
fugitive scientists and technicians will teach the guerrillas
incredible tactics and skills. He predicts that the West,
deprived of its technical advantage, will invade South
America and Africa in latter-day crusades thus meeting the
guerrillas on their own ground and repeating the mistake
of Vietnam. He predicts that the West will be totally de-
feated by the end of the 29th century. He predicts that
the guerrillas will destroy every vestige of the old economy
based on mass production and consumption. He predicts
a new economy dedicated to transcending the human level
of performance in all fields. As to the steps necessary to
achieve this victory he writes: "He who opposes force
with counterforce alone forms that which he opposes and
is formed by it. History shows that when a system of
government is overthrown by force a system in many respects similar will take place. On the other hand he who
does not resist force that enslaves and exterminates will be
enslaved and exterminated. For revolution to effect basic
changes in existing conditions three tactics are required:
1. Disrupt. 2. Attack. 3. Disappear. Look away. Ignore.
Forget. These three tactics to be employed *alternatively*."

So he enunciated the concept of My Own Business
units consisting of like-minded individuals forming sepa-

rate communities. "The MOBs must be camouflaged to survive. For example MOB takes over apartment building from mortgage to janitor, now another next door, now a whole block on the surface perfectly normal stupid folk. Or MOB takes over small town sheriff, jail and bank. No beards no long hair just an ordinary small town.

"New concepts can only arise when one achieves a measure of disengagement from enemy conditions. On the other hand disengagement is difficult in a concentration camp is it not?. . .1. Disrupt. . . Fifty young men record riot sound effects on portable tape recorders. They strap the recorders under gabardine topcoats. They hit the rush hour recorders on full blast screams, police whistles, breaking glass, crunch of night sticks, tear gas flapping from their clothes. . .2. Attack in subsequent confusion. . .3. Retire to MOB. Learn Chinese. . . Disrupt again. . . Attack . . . Disappear. Look away. Ignore. Forget."

Q : You have described America as a nightmare. Would you enlarge on this point?

A : America is not so much a nightmare as a non-dream. The American non-dream is precisely a move to wipe the dream out of existence. The dream is a spontaneous happening and therefore dangerous to a control system set up by the non-dreamers. Experiments carried out by Doctor Gross in New York at the Mount Sinai Hospital indicate that any dream in the male is accompanied by erection. The non-dream program is specifically directed against the male principle. It is above all anti-sexual and anti-male.

Any progress or system of thought must have ground to grow on and especially such a vegetable program as this dead hand stretching the vegetable people. The ground for the non-dream program was well laid by the turn of the century, ready for seeds which would yield in course of time hideous fruit. World Wars I, II, and III were already inevitable, given the basic formula of nationalism. The concomitant rise of communism would serve as pretext for more control measures while the communists would be driven to apply similar measures and thus serve the master plan. Let us look at some of the milestones in the anti-dream plan:

The Oriental Exclusion Acts: The equanimity of the Chinese is, of course, due to their language which allows for periods of silence and *undirected* thought, quite intolerable to the non-dreamers who must program *all* thought. I have already spoken of the difference between hieroglyphic and syllabic writing. (If I hold up a sign on which the word "ROSE" is written, you *must* repeat the word sub-vocally. If I hold up a hieroglyphic sign for rose you do not have to repeat the word, and even have the option of silence.) Admittedly, two model control systems, the Mayan and the Egyptian, were based on hieroglyphic writing. However, these control systems were predicated on the illiteracy of the controlled. Universal literacy with a concomitant control of word and image is now the instrument of control. An essential feature of the Western control machine is to make language as *non-pictorial* as possible, to separate words as far as possible from objects or observable processes.

The District Supervisor shabby office late afternoon shadow in his eyes calm and grey as a wise old rat handed a typed page across the desk

Relations between human beings sexualizing congruent accessibility ambivalently fecundate with orifices perspectives is I feel to beg the question of contributory latent configurations reciprocally starved of direction or vector by the recognizable human remembrance of such approximate exasperations a desperately effete societal somnolence supine negation by any reputable informed latent consensus inherently commissioned with customary human techniques interweaving re-enactments of necessary correspondences interderivational from complementary internalizations confluently communicated reciprocal analogous metaphors with this relentlessly successful diagrammatic schemata delinquently recognizable juxtapositions to traduce or transfigure a pulsating multiplicity of contradictions inherent in linguistic engagements disproportionately

flailing gritty colloquialisms edged with grammatic outrage bubbling beneath indispensably internalized concordance latterly derivative from scorned or pillage infantile
suburban genitalia sexualizing exasperations into diagrammatically contrapunctual linguistically communicated
multiplicity of otherness escalating the delinquent preparations in concomitantly banal privatization concentrates
of irrelevant hysteria contributory misinformed perspectives of negation ambivalently supine oppositionally interweaving desperately recognizable latterly commissioned
flailing stridently illiterate human beings would traduce or
transfigure fecundate with orifices potentials reputably
informed correspondences of societal consensus notwithstanding the complementary structuralized configurations
relentlessly juxtapositions interdependence of necessary
and precisely reciprocal consensus latterly contingent
upon communicated linguistic concordance of such contractually analogous indispensably infantile preparations
fecundately accessible human correspondences or relations
between human internalized concordance indispensably
starved of direction or vector by irrelevant approximately
derivative confluent exasperations latently misinformed
contingent inaccessibility communicated societal internal-
izings indispensably pillaged infantile preparations flailing disproportionate bubbling outrage notwithstanding the
contrapoised stridently juxtapositions interdependence
latterly commissioned recognizable societally structuralized
reciprocally misinformed indispensably congruent multiplicity of otherness perspectives concomitantly banal
irrelevant concentrates with orifices gritty interstices
rectilinearally inaccessible.

These jewels gathered from one of the periodicals
admittedly subsidized by the CIA. If you see the function
of word as extension of our senses to witness and experience through the writer's eyes then this may be dubbed
blind prose. It sees nothing and neither does the reader.
Not an image in a cement mixer of this word paste. As a
literary exercise I pick up the Penguin translation of
Rimbaud and select images to place in congruent juxta-

positions with this colorless vampiric prose which having no color of its own must steal color from the readers such contractually accessible linguistically structuralized preparations on blue evenings I shall go down the path in a dream feeling the coolness on my feet starved of direction or vector by derivationally confluent exasperations five in the evening at the Green Inn huge beer mug froth turned into gold by a ray of late sunshine perspective of illiterate human beings would traduce or transfigure fecundate with orifices potential the Watchman rows through the luminous heavens and from his flaming dragnet lets fall shooting stars and precisely reciprocal latent consensus if societal flailings stridently congruent from pulsating mangrove swamps riddled with pools and water snakes digrammatic contrapunctual. . .ving desperately the poverty of image shea. . .in bronze from scorned or pillage consensus of contributory configurations. . .like a flock of doves shivering of Venetian blinds and the yellow blue awakening sexualizing contingent accessibility informed hideous wrecks at the bottom of brown gulfs where the giant snakes devoured by lice fall from the twisted trees with black odors communicated suburban orifice re-enactments of infantile genitalia contributory internalized contradictions blue waves golden singing fish foam of shadow flowers would traduce or transfigure banal privatization concentrates latterly risen from violet fogs through the wall of the reddening sky ambivalently supine contractually inaccessible black cold pool where a child squatting full of sadness launches a boat fragile as a butterfly in May between starved confluent exasperations communicated linear derivations from reciprocal engagements spat blood concomitantly irrelevant hysteria at the foot of dark walls beating the skinny dogs internalized vector misinformed preparation it is raining softly on the town moonlight as the clock was striking twelve concentrates of otherness with orifices bitter perspectives the road without sound is white under the empty moon a slight cesspool of dirty blood internalized infantile diagrammatically necessary piercing cry in the darkened square spat blood confluently

stinging like the salt of child's tears sexualizing interdependence latterly contingent upon a motionless boat in
ashen waters concordantly infantile misinformed perspectives North wind across the wreckage perish power justice
vanish ambivalently supine fecundately human there are
brothers dark strangers if we began bubbling beneath indispensably banal privatization concentrates blond soldiers from the thin bracken the wilderness the meadows
the horizon are washing themselves red in the storm
delinquently pulsating oppositional colonnades under blue
light railway stations wind from the sky threw sheets of ice
across the ponds vector latterly communicated the question of internalized direction at four o'clock on a summer
morning the sleep of love the wind comes in to wander
about under the bed reputably such contractually accessible human concordance is I feel to beg the question then
they will have to deal with the crafty rat ghastly will-o'-the-
wisp comes like a gunshot after vespers configurations of
internalized congruencies

Saharan blue where a thousand blue devils dance in the
air like flowers of fire supine oppositionally pillaged
inaccessible jackals howling across deserts of thyme stridently misinformed preparations communicated the question of pillaged consensus it is raining internalized concordance dawn rising like a flock of doves softly on the
town shivering of Venetian blinds at four o'clock and the
yellow blue awakening concentrates the sleep of love on
orifices summer accessibility the skinny dogs internalized
flowers of fire

Anything they can do you can do better. Pick up *The
Concise Oxford Dictionary* mix your own linguistic virus
concentrates fire burn and caldron bubble mix it black and
mix it strong folks hereabouts have done you wrong return confluently the complement: e.

Fristic elite impacted banal limitrophic imposture im-
potently flailing effluvial grout mud incumbent MN
grume intervolving abrasively affricative incubus inter-
positional inconsummate lubricious investiture decom-
missioned externalized incondite anastrophe incrassate

misinformed ME palatogram's epidemic anfractuosity
eschatological obscurant retiary disaffected lumper uxorious urubu anachronic prologist consensual nevermore
bubbling beneath innavigable umlaut inextricably dis-
admeasured societal interstices reciprocally ablative
inconditely flailing oppositional contagonist precatory ingravescent gowk disobliged catoptic zillah pillaged
consensus of justiciable justiciar kempy kavass libating
opponency orifices adventitious encumbrancer anachronic
hysteria of vector its heart misinformed pulp irrefrangible
disaffected echidna encounter ineluctable obmutescence
arachnoid troglodyte flailing inofficious effluvium disobliged
investiture rectilinear additive disadhesion impacted limitrophic elite irrefrangible contagonist anachronic uxorious
troglodyte sexualizing ingravescent propinquities intervolving abrasive innocupation congruently disinternalized necessities ill informed pulp extrapolating diagrammatic
efferent prehensions obmutescent palatogram's prefigured
eschatologist uxoriously disobliged investiture nevermore
bubbling beneath innavigable effluvium impotent obloquy
irrefrangible hysteria such additive ineluctable disadhesion
irrefrangible limitrophic incubus bubbling uxorious pulp
ablative palatogram precatory impacted adhesion effluvial
inconsummate lubricious flailings ingravescent contagonist
retiary umlaut prefigured eristic eschatologist, *voici le
temps des assassins* blind man's bluff any number can
play...blind prose but it has direction and purpose. One
purpose is to protect a camouflaged thesis from the em-
barrassment of factual testing. If I say "England is an
island" I can produce evidence to support my statement
should anyone call it in question. If they write an article
attacking the Olympia Press as sexualizing congruent accessibility to its heart of pulp fecundate with orifices perspectives in the name of human privacy they have placed
their thesis beyond the realm of fact since the words used
refer to nothing that can be tested. The words used refer
to nothing. The words used have no referent.

The Oriental Exclusion Acts blocked a dangerous influx and
laid the ground for future conflicts. The program calls for a

series of such conflicts to point up the need for a continual escalation of control measures.

Income-tax Laws: These laws benefit those who are already rich. The richer you are the easier it is to minimize taxes. In effect the rich have closed the doors to extreme wealth. This is necessary to insure that no one acquires wealth who might use it to subvert the interests of wealth and monopoly. There is no tighter hierarchy than extreme wealth, and no one gets in who is not devoted to the interests of money.

Passport and customs controls after World War I: The basic formula on which the control plan depends is *unilateral communication.* Everyone must be forced to receive communications from the control machine. It will readily be seen that any control measure expands the range of enforced communication. Your passport or visa is not quite in order? You have lost your currency control slip? How many times will you compulsively repeat the explanation you have prepared in case the customs official starts asking questions. So control measures conjure up phantom interrogators who invade and destroy your inner freedom.

By far the most crucial milestone in the non-dream plan was the Harrison Narcotics Act.

Q : *Does total destruction seem to you a desirable outcome?*

A : I would say total destruction of existing institutions, and very rapidly, may be the only alternative to a nuclear war which would be very much more destructive. If disorder reaches a certain point, they will not be able to start a nuclear war, which I think is very definitely and obviously the intention of the people in power. Certainly in America—they absolutely intend to start a nuclear war. A bomb on New York would solve a lot of their problems. Remember that most of the opposition to the machine is concentrated in the large cities. I think they're quite willing to risk a nuclear war. However, they won't even be able to do that if the entire structure falls apart. Of the two, I certainly prefer the total destruction of the present system of society to a nuclear war, which is the inevitable result of its remaining in operation.

three
A new frog

Q : *Does sexuality play an important role in your work?*

A : Yes.

Q : *Do you distinguish between the erotic, the sexual, and the pornographic?*

A : All these words are loaded with hidden meanings. For example, pornography is a double-barreled word, it has an unfavorable implication, within the word itself. So, given the fact that the words themselves are completely confused, I can't distinguish between them. The distinction between eroticism and sexuality, for example—I think this is another case of the either-or in Western thought: it's either love or sex. . . I think what we're dealing with here is largely verbal confusion which is implicit in these words.

Q : *In your work, eroticism has become a gigantic machine which destroys itself. Does your eroticism lead to something else, does it have another meaning, or is it the expression of destruction?*

A : Well, I could answer that with a question. . . We don't know enough to know; we don't know what eroticism is, we don't know what sex is, we don't know why it's pleasurable, and the reason why we don't know these things is that it's such a highly charged area no one can look at it . . . The idea of any scientific investigation throws people into puritanical convulsions. There's just no objectivity possible. I would say that if we really understood something about eroticism—what sex is, why sex is pleasurable (it's obviously an electromagnetic phenomenon; Reich has measured it actually). . .and as to where it would lead. . .well, it might possibly lead to some basic recognition.

Q : *What "erotic" or "pornographic" writers seem important to you?*

A : I object once again to the words erotic or pornographic. I'd simply refer to writers who've written more or less explicitly or frankly about sexual matters. Well, certainly Genet. I realize the importance of de Sade but I find it very dull reading. Certainly Joyce, Miller, and D. H. Lawrence were very important as pioneers and made some very important breakthroughs, so that now virtually anything can be published.

Q : *There is an evident parallel between your work and that of Hieronymous Bosch. No one would think of saying that Bosch is pornographic. The most prudish and "respectable" people regard Bosch's paintings with unconscious admiration, while reading one page of yours would scandalize them. What is the source of this inconsistency in judgment?*

A : There are a number of sources. In the first place, the respectable person doesn't see what's going on in Bosch at all. They don't realize that things are going on there that are precisely what I described in *Naked Lunch:* they don't see it. Also, it's old; that's very important. Respectable people can go look at Priapic statues without being upset because they're in museums. They are old. Henry Miller, I believe, pointed that out in one of his articles. It's just another example of the complete irrational schizophrenia of the thought processes of so-called respectable people. Something's in a museum and it's famous and it's old, so it is all right. There's also a difference between painting and writing of course.

Q : *There is a sexual ritual in your work which often leads to a human sacrifice. Does the civilization suppress its sacrifices and its sexually oriented rites?*

A : Well, yes, I would say that they haven't eliminated them, they've simply suppressed the overt manifestations of such rites. Now the Aztecs were quite overt in their human sacrifices: we are not, but we go in and destroy races as we've destroyed the Indians, as the terrible Boers

destroyed the Bushmen, and the Australian settlers destroyed the Australian aborigines. The destruction is more
widespread. It has no ritual significance, but it amounts
to even more destruction in human terms than would be
brought about by actual human sacrifices. On the other
hand, of course, I am not for one minute suggesting that
these rather disgusting, silly rites be reinstituted; no one
could really take them very seriously any more: Dust of
the dead gods.

Q : *The sex act often arrives in your work as a movement of
universal fornication, in which all living things, sometimes even those from another planet, participate. What
are the meaning and the importance of that vision?*

A : Well, as to the importance of it, I wouldn't be able to
say. It is simply a perception that sex is a very widespread
phenomenon in the interconnection of living matter and
non-living matter as well.

Q : *Carl, in* The Soft Machine, *is coated with gelatin, his
body is placed in a female mold which slowly transforms
him. Can this transformation apply to contemporary man?*

A : Even on a scientific level we're very near being able to
make all sorts of alterations in the human body. They
are now able to replace the parts, like on an old car
when it runs down. The next thing, of course, will be
transplanting of brains. We presume that the ego, what
we call the ego, the I, or the You, is located somewhere
in the midbrain, so it's not very long before we can transfer an ego from one body to another. Rich men will be
able to buy up young bodies. Many of the passages in my
work, that were purely fanciful at the time, are now quite
within the range of possibility.

Q : *Orgasm is often bound up with death in the numerous
hangings which one encounters in your work. What is the
connection between orgasm and death?*

A : This is a very obscure question. Many people who've considered the evidence do believe that we have lived other lives. The possible connection would be that a person dies in the orgasm in which he is born—he dies into his own conception, as it were; and that would be the continuity involved. Freud referred to the orgasm as "*la petite mort*"—the little death. It is a moment of unconsciousness, in some cases, that approximates some of the manifestations of death. Of course, orgasm may occur at the moment of death, as in hanging, cyanide poisoning, and various convulsive states; also, it's quite a common cause of death in cardiac patients. It's worse than running up six flights of stairs, and many women have been embarrassed to find that their old sugar daddy has conked out on them. You know, "Died in so-and-so's apartment..." I don't want to mention several people, but you know, it's sort of like "Killed While Cleaning His Gun"...

Q : *In The Soft Machine two characters are split in half and rejoined to make two new persons. What is the symbolism of that union?*

A : Well, the human body actually is two halves. The two halves are not similar. The left side and the right side are not similar, not only because most people use their right hand more. The right side of the brain, if you are right-handed, is practically unused. There's quite a difference between the right side of your face and the left side of your face. Someone recently made up some pictures taking both right sides of people's faces, and then both left sides, and they looked quite different. So, you could take two people, split one person down the middle and put that half over onto another person and make new people that way. There's no particular symbolism. It's just a possibility which I imagine in the course of time might be in the reach of medical science. They're getting to be quite competent mechanics, I'll say that for them.

Q : Hanging is also a sort of alchemy which effects the transfer of a thought into another body at the moment of ejaculation. What does this represent?

A : It might represent possibly the transfer of the ego into another body at the moment of ejaculation. This possibility I've explored more fully in *The Soft Machine*. But it really is sort of outdated now, because the whole thing can be done surgically. They just take the brain— take Hearst's brain and clap it into another body; that's what he always wanted. All these old characters who refuse to die... It might be regarded as a rather primitive attempt of transfer of an ego from one body to another.

Q : What is the importance of sadism in your work?

A : There's not that much sadism. While I have that reputation, I don't think I dwell very much on torture with a sexual connotation. It certainly is nothing that interests me personally; beating people, being beaten, all that just seems to me terribly dull and unpleasant.

Q : The sexual acts which you describe seem to be subject to precise physical laws, series of contacts which release certain mechanisms. Sometimes, even bare nerves are caressed. Do you conceive the sexual relations of your characters as purely mechanical reflexes?

A : Obviously, the human body itself is a very complex machine, which does not mean that you are your body. Because a body doesn't move of itself; it's made of very much the same material as this table, and we wouldn't expect this table to move of itself, it's a very complicated machine which is occupied by someone in the capacity of a very incompetent pilot. Now, there's no question but what sexual stimulation could be caused by direct electrical manipulation of nerve centers, etc., just as any machine can be manipulated—it *is* a machine. In particular, the sexual aspects of the machine we know very little about simply because there's no research, because no research is allowed. This is one of the most important aspects of the monopoly of vested interests: They must stimulate sex, and make sex difficult to obtain. In that way, they keep people always thinking about it, always worrying about it, and it keeps them from causing trouble.

Q : The connection between sex and color recurs several times and seems to fascinate you. Why?

A : Once again, you see, what I am attempting to do is to derive some approximation of some of the laws and facts about sex—what it—what it is and how it works. Unquestionably, there is a relationship between sex and color. That is, sexual color photos are much more sexually stimulating than black-and-white pictures. These, of course, are available to everyone now with the new Polaroid color cameras. I imagine people are taking pictures of themselves right and left. Not without danger... I've known people to make themselves very sick that way. You're dealing with something you don't know very much about. It's a tricky area.

Q : There are few women in your books. When they do appear, it's Mary, in The Soft Machine, who eats the genitals of Johnny, whom she's just hanged... Or it's the constipated American housewife who is afraid her mixmaster will get under her skirts while she is waiting for the washing machine to finish its cycle. How do you feel about women?

A : In the words of one of a great misogynist's plain Mr Jones, in Conrad's Victory: "Women are a perfect curse." I think they were a basic mistake, and the whole dualistic universe evolved from this error. Women are no longer essential to reproduction as this article indicates:

OXFORD SCIENTISTS REPRODUCE FROGS FROM SINGLE CELLS
By Walter Sullivan

Oxford, England, Oct. 8 (NYT).—Experimenters at Oxford University believe they have removed all doubt about the validity of experiments in which frogs have been produced from single cells extracted from another frog.

The experiments in what is known as vegetative reproduction bear on one of the most fundamental problems in biology—namely, what it is that turns on and turns off the genetic material buried within each cell of the body.

The frogs, according to the experiments, have been produced from cells that line the intestine. This has demonstrated that even such highly specialized cells contain, within their nuclei, the information needed to construct an entire new individual. Normally such information lies dormant, but in the Oxford experiments it has been activated.

Skeptics' Argument

Until now, some scientists have believed that, in such specialized cells, the genetic information unrelated to that cell's function has been permanently erased. Those skeptical of the Oxford experiments, under way for several years, argued that the frogs raised here grew from non-specialized cells that somehow made their way into the intestine.

However, Dr John Gurden of Oxford, in charge of the research, said it was now evident that this could not be so because more than 30 percent of the intestinal cells can be made to grow at least to the polliwog stage.

This, he said, is incompatible with the idea that these polliwogs have grown from rarely occurring non-specialized cells. Only 1 or 2 percent of the cells grow to full mature and fertile frogs, but this, in Dr Gurden's view, is because of subtle damage to the cell nucleus during manipulation.

The experiments have created a sensation here because they imply that, in theory if not in practice, it should be

possible to mass-produce identical twins of people gifted
with exceptional ability or beauty.

Dr Gurden has struggled to dissociate himself from
such speculation. His goal, he said, is to understand how
the genetic information in a body cell is controlled.

While the nucleus of a cell lining a man's intestine
contains all the information needed to produce an identical twin, only one tiny bit of that information is active.

It says: "You are an intestinal liner; you must grow in
a certain way and perform certain chemical functions."

What Dr Gurden and his co-workers have done is to
take such a nucleus from the intestine of a tadpole and
implant it inside a frog egg whose own nucleus had been
destroyed, Something in the material of the egg—the
cytoplasm—tells that nucleus: "You are no longer an intestinal cell nucleus, you are an egg cell nucleus; go to
work." The result, if all goes well, is a new frog.

Q : For Antonin Artaud, sexuality is a barrier to the rapprochement of men and women. What do you think?

A : I'm not interested in this rapprochement. I don't see it
as a barrier; I think that the whole anti-sex orientation
of our society is basically manipulated by female interests.
Because it is to their interest to keep sexuality down;
that's the way they hang onto a man, or latch on to one,
and then he's not supposed to do anything else. It is the
vested interest of the female sex, which is anti-sexual.

Q : In your books, emotions between people who unite
sexually do not exist.

A : I wouldn't say that emotions between people who unite
sexually don't exist. In the book I'm writing now there's a
considerable amount of emotion. I think that what we
call love is a fraud perpetrated by the female sex, and
that the point of sexual relations between men is nothing
that we could call love, but rather what we might call
recognition.

Q : What is the symbolism of the lesbian agents with penises grafted onto their faces, drinking spinal fluid?

A : Oh, just a bit of science fiction, really.

Q : What causes the fear and anxiety which some people experience when authors whom they consider "pornographic" are brought up?

A : The general fear of sexuality, of course. A fear that is carefully fostered by their upbringing and training, which is basically controlled by women. If they weren't afraid of it, they'd find out more about it, and if they found out more about it, this would be a considerable threat to all vested interests.

Q : You have said that the family is one of the principal obstacles to any real human progress. Why?

A : In the first place, it means that children are brought up by women. In the second place, it means that any sort of nonsense that the parents suffer from—any neuroses or confusions—are immediately passed on to the helpless child. Everyone seems to consider that parents have every right to inflict on their children any sort of pernicious nonsense from which they themselves suffer, and which was passed on to them in turn by their parents, so that the whole human race is crippled in childhood, and this is done by the family. More than that, nations, and countries, are merely an extension of the family, and if any formula is really holding the world back, it's the formula of nations, countries, which, as I say, is merely an extension of the biologic family. We aren't going to get anywhere at all until this ridiculous unit is disbanded.

There are a number of ways to do that. Of course, there's the most obvious, which is for the children to be removed from their biologic parents at birth, and brought up in sort of state nurseries. This has been proposed often, but there again you have to consider what sort of training and environment they have in the state nurseries.

Another suggestion, by Mr Brion Gysin, is that children should be paid to go to school. In other words, the further they advance in education the more money they get. This, from a very early age, would begin to break down their economic dependence on their parents, and, say, when a boy graduated from a university, he would have enough money to start his career without relying on his parents. The real thing that keeps children tied to their parents is economic dependence, and this must be broken down.

Q : There have already been several attempts to eliminate the family, but they have not borne fruit. Why have they failed?

A : Well, for one thing, they didn't go far enough. I imagine China may have come closer to it than any other country, though I haven't had an opportunity to see what's going on there. Russia pretended they were going to do it, and then did nothing about it; the same old bourgeois family apparently exists in Russia as we have in the Western world. Of course the people with vested interest in the family are women. Obviously, any attempt to attack the family has them frothing at the mouth.

Q : What would be necessary to replace the family?

A : Nothing. Nothing. I don't see there's any need for the family at all. For example, you start off this way. Artificial insemination, of course, is now quite possible. All right, you pick your donors and your women, the women become pregnant, they're kept in a hospital till the baby's born— don't want them wandering around, because there's all sorts of things that can happen to a child before birth. Another thing very important is that there should be no noise when the child is born; no one should say anything, because those words at that very traumatic instant leave a permanent impression. Mr L. Ron Hubbard, the founder of Scientology, says that during any period of unconsciousness it is absolutely criminal for anyone to say anything, because those words are imprinted in the organism, and if they are restimulated or repeated later, the pain will be re-experienced, and they're very crippling. O.K., the baby is born, then it's transferred to a nursery, or whatever, to be raised. That's all. . . No family.

Q : Do you think we will arrive, or have already arrived at the point of creating artificial beings without recourse to normal reproductive processes? Does that seem desirable to you?

A : I think it's quite within the range of modern technology, and it seems very desirable to me indeed, because it would bring about elimination of the family. But research along these lines is blocked, of course, by vested interests, and particularly by the vested interest of the female sex; their monopoly is the baby thing. Now, if you could produce artificial beings, you could produce them at a reasonable age, and you wouldn't have all this infancy. Yes, it seems to me very desirable.

Q : What connection is there between drugs and homosexuality?

A : None whatsoever that I can see. I mean, any organism is subject to the effects of drugs, human or animal; there seems to be no relation between drugs and homosexuality, or heterosexuality.

Q : Now, do drugs affect perception of sexual experience?

A : It depends upon the drugs. Some of the hallucinogenic drugs have certain aphrosdisiac properties; they increase awareness, and therefore may increase awareness of sexual experience. Opiates, of course, are completely antisexual. The idea you get from idiotic press talk about drug addicts committing rape—(they're incapable of getting an erection, have no interest in sex whatever: a heroin addict is no more interested in sex than an old turnip)—is absolutely a misconception. Cocaine and benzedrine have some aphrosdisiac properties. All the sedative drugs are antisexual—alcohol, barbiturates, tranquilizers depress the sexual impulse.

Q : *A.J. is obliged to call his bodyguards to get him away from the American women in rut who fall upon him. What do you think of American women?*

A : I think they're possibly one of the worst expressions of the female sex because they've been allowed to go further. This whole worship of women that flourished in the Old South, and in frontier days, when there weren't many, is still basic in American life; and the whole Southern worship of women and white supremacy is still the policy of America. They lost the Civil War, but their policies still dominate America. It's a matriarchal, white supremacist country. There seems to be a very definite link between matriarchy and white supremacy.

Q : *The orgone theory of Doctor Wilhelm Reich is mentioned several times in your work. What importance do you attach to it?*

A : I think it's a tremendously important discovery, perhaps not as important as Doctor Reich thought, but certainly something that warrants a good deal of investigation. And the fact that it's been so viciously suppressed by the Federal Pure Food and Drug Administration in America is an indication, I think, of its importance. You can almost judge the importance of a discovery by the efforts made to suppress it. Reich's Orgone Theory is an example of a discovery that was very viciously suppressed ...the apomorphine treatment for drug addiction is another.

four
Academy 23

Q : *Do you think that the creation of a center of practical and theoretical sexual research could help fathom the still-obscure laws of sexuality?*

A : Unquestionably. I think in very few years that would lead to a very basic breakthrough. . .there's never been any real research. Well, there was a project in St. Louis, Missouri, where they took color pictures of people having sexual intercourse—from 18 to 80—which I presume that nobody can see unless they're researchers, or something of the sort. They found out very little as far as I can make out.

Q : *Is there, in the still very strong opposition against eroticism, in art as in life, a manifestation of the control of consciousness?*

A : Oh, unquestionably, it's the most important point of control. They lose control of that, and they really lose control. And they're determined not to lose control.

Q : *How do you envision the future of relations between men and women?*

A : In *The Soft Machine:* I proposed that the sexes be separated, that all male children be raised by males and all female children be raised by women. The less the two sexes have to do with each other, the better, I think.

Q : *Well, then you wouldn't need women any more, would you, as soon as it was all being done automatically?*

A : No, perhaps that's assuming you could have wombs in bottles, so that there wouldn't be any need for these women. . .

INSTITUTE OF ADVANCED SEXUAL STUDIES ACADEMY BULLETIN
No. 18

The uh aim of the institute is to examine uh sexual manifestations with the same objective and uh experimental operations as have yielded such marked results in

the uh physical sciences. We cannot but be impressed
by the inefficiency of the present arrangement, the long
period of helpless infancy during which the child is exposed to every variety of physical and psychic illness,
every unwholesome influence on set. It is precisely our
aim to create children at a reasonable age with some
immunity against the unfortunate influences that we cannot immediately control. Meanwhile, every effort must
be made to crack the biologic family unit. It is no exaggeration to say that the family unit, with its drearily predictable yield of infantile trauma, the quite unnecessary
tensions of modern life superimposed on these quite unnecessary wounds, is the most crippling basic factor in
modern life. How many potentially talented and useful
citizens do nothing throughout a lifetime but protest
against early conditioning? It has frequently been proposed
that children be brought up by the state. And what is
the state but a simple extension of the tribe which in
turn is an extension of the family? To shift the care of
children from the private family to the state family is
nothing to the purpose. This means that our children
will surface in a straitjacket of dogmatic verbal formulation as is now imposed by the biologic family. One of the
most promising suggestions for the long-term liquidation
of the family problem has been proposed by Mr Brion
Gysin. He suggests that children be paid to go to school;
the allowance increasing as they advance in training, they
progressively achieve economic freedom from the family.
The solution of the family problem must be termed a
prerequisite for any objective approach to sexual manifestations and phenomena. Our work has been hamstrung
by the antisex monopolist power, because this might lead
to a basic understanding of the mechanisms involved
with concomitant freedom from early conditioning. The
doctor asked his subjects to wear transparent plastic suits,
and observed whether dreaming was overtly sexual or not.
One wonders to what extent the content of dreams could

be dictated by cutting in at very short intervals certain words and images? Since the results of this experiment are well known to all of us, suffice it to say such experiments have been carried out, relative to such basic and uh predictable factors... I refer to experiments that did not uh pan out as we had anticipated. Science, pure science. You learn to take what comes in this business.

"How's that couple coming along in double emersion tank No. 187?"

"Don't look at it, boss, it's too horrible. They're melting together, and one is eating the other inside."

"*Selbstverstandlich*," snapped the Herr Doktor. "And vat did you think would happen, so stupid American swine?"

At this point, a most regrettable brawl broke out in the operation room, overturning nutrient tanks, jars, aquariums, sloshing monstrous larval being across the floor the scientists slip about slashing at each other with scalpels and bone saws screaming.

"Well, we got the orders, and I done the job, wife and kids on my back."

"Look what a *dumnheit*."

"Smells through the outhouse, doctor."

"Run for it, chaps. They're actives." Last seen swimming desperately in erogenous sewage.

The entire project was lost. Who is the manager here? You see what I mean?... Such knowledge in the wrong hands could be quite unfortunate!

Q : We spoke of power and its disastrous consequences; now we come to drugs. Is it a power device?

A : It seems to me that drugs are one of the ideal power devices. The so-called drug problem is a pretext—thin, and getting thinner—to extend police power over areas of actual or potential opposition. In Western countries, opposition is concentrated in the 18-to-25 age group. So, make more drug laws, publicize all drug news, and a good percentage of the opposition is criminal by legal definition. According to an article in *Life* magazine (July 24, 1967), authorities estimate as many as ten million Americans have tried marijuana at least once, and that the number of users is increasing rapidly. Of course, they can't put ten million people in jail—that would be coming too far out into the open. If there's one thing Western authorities don't want to do, it's come out into the open with what they're doing. But they can keep young people under continual threat of police search or action, at the same time divert rebellion into the dead-end channels of addiction and criminality. Authority in the West has never been more threatened than it is right now, and after the manner of its parasitic species reacts with hysterical rage. Reactionary authority does not hesitate to brand as criminal anyone who publicly favors the legalization of marijuana or even ventures to point out that heroin and cannabis do not belong under the same legal, or even pharmaceutical definition. I'll give you an example of that:

> *Doctor Calls Mick Jagger Criminal for Urging Freedom of Drug-taking.* Geneva, Aug. 3 (UPI)—Canadian physician, Dr. Paul Campbell, today classed as "criminals" those people who advocated the drug L.S.D. Dr. Campbell also strongly attacked British pop singer, Mick Jagger, of the Rolling Stones, for allegedly stating that people should be free to take drugs if they wish.
> The Canadian doctor addressed an assembly on drug-taking of the Moral Rearmament Group at its headquarters in Caux.

Q : *I think it is necessary to establish the difference between the different types of drugs and hallucinogens. How can one categorize them in terms of their physiological effects?*

A : This is a quotation from an address given to the American Psychological Society in 1961: "Unfortunately, the word drug activates a reflex of fear, disapproval, and prurience in Western nervous systems." Drug, of course, is simply a generic term for any chemical agent. Alcohol is a sedative drug, similar in action to the barbiturates; yet, because of purely verbal associations, we do not think of alcohol as being a drug, because it is our national drug.

The American Narcotics Department has bracketed substances with opposite physiological effects as narcotic drugs. Morphine is actually an antidote for cocaine poisoning; cannabis is an hallucinogenic drug with no chemical or physiological affinity to either cocaine or morphine. Yet, cocaine, morphine and cannabis are all classified as narcotic drugs. Unquestionably the term has emotional impact; but, used in such a loose fashion, it has no useful precision of meaning. I would like to draw, at the outset, a clear distinction between sedatives and hallucinogenic agents, between addicting and non-addicting drugs.

What is addiction? The use of opium or derivatives leads to a state which limits and describes addiction. The morphine or heroin addict provides a model and mirror of addiction. The addict functions on heroin: without it he is as helpless as a beached fish, out of his medium. This situation of total dependence did not exist prior to his contact with heroin, and his subsequent addiction. A month, more or less, of daily exposure through injection or sniffing the drug, and the addict is hooked—that is, addicted for life. Even if the addict is cured and off the drug for years, he can be readdicted by one or two shots ... Like the alcoholic, he has acquired a lifelong sensitivity to the drug.

Investigators still do not know how heroin addiction is contracted. Dr Isbell of Lexington, Kentucky, where most U.S. addicts are treated, has suggested that morphine acts on the cell receptors, perhaps altering the molecular structure of certain cell groups in the body.

While the action of morphine is not fully understood, alcohol and barbiturates are definite front-brain sedatives, and increased doses are generally required to achieve sedation. In fact, all sedative drugs may be said to act by sedating—that is, putting out of action some function of the nervous system, by decreasing awareness of surroundings and bodily processes. Addiction wouldn't seem to be a prerogative of sedatives, and perhaps the opiates are the only class of truly addicting drugs. The symptoms that follow barbiturate withdrawal may be regarded as a mechanical reaction to massive front-brain sedation, rather than biologic need for the drug.

What is a hallucinogen? A drug that expands consciousness and increases awareness of surroundings and bodily processes. I would suggest the term consciousness-expanding drug be substituted for hallucinogen, because, for one thing, it is very difficult to pronounce. Actual hallucinations are rare, and no precise definition of a hallucination has been formulated. Under the influence of LSD, mescaline, cannabis, the subject is acutely aware of colors, sounds, odors, and the effect of the drug may be said to consist in this phenomenon of increased awareness, which may be pleasant or unpleasant, depending on the content of the awareness. Colors and sounds gain an intense meaning and many insights carry over after the drug effects have worn off. Under the influence of mescaline, I have had the experience of seeing a painting for the first time, and I found later that I could see the painting without using the drug. The same insights into music, the beauty of an object, ordinarily ignored, carry over so that one exposure to a powerful consciousness-expanding drug often conveys a permanent increase in the range of experience. Mescaline transports the user to unexplored psychic areas, and he can often find the way back without a chemical guide. I will describe a simple experiment that will make the distinction between sedative and consciousness-expanding drugs more precise. As

far as I know, this experiment has not been carried out
in detail. Here is the proposed experiment: Administer
a consciousness-expanding drug together with a precise
array of stimuli—music, pictures, odors, tastes . . . timed
and recorded, so that the entire battery of stimuli can
be repeated in exact sequence.

Some days later, when the effects of the drug are completely dissipated, expose the subject to the same stimuli,
in the same order. To what extent is the hallucinogen
experience reactivated?

Everyone who has used the consciousness-expanding
drugs knows that any one stimulus, experienced under
the influence of the drug, can reactivate the drug experience. There is every reason to believe that the drug
experience could be recaptured in detail with precise
repetition of associated stimuli.

Now try the same experiment with a morphine addict;
administer a dose of morphine together with a battery
of stimuli; wait until withdrawal symptoms occur. Now
repeat the stimuli. Is any relief from withdrawal symptoms experienced? On the contrary, the associated stimuli
reactivate and intensify the need for the drug. The same,
of course, is true of alcohol. Stimuli associated with the
consumption of alcohol reactivate the need for alcohol,
and conduce to relapse.

The use of sedative drugs leads to increased dependence on the drug used. The use of consciousness-expanding drugs could show the way to obtain the useful aspects
of hallucinogenic experience, without any chemical
agent. Anything that can be done chemically can be done
in other ways, with sufficient knowledge of the mechanisms involved. Recently, a Cambridge dentist has extracted teeth with no other anesthetic than music through
headphones. The consciousness-expanding experience can
be induced by flicker—that is, rhythmic light flashing in
the retina at the rate of from ten to twenty-five flashes
per second. (I quote from Gray Walter's *The Living*

Brain)—"The rhythmic series of flashes appear to be breaking down some of the physiologic barriers between different regions of the brain. This means the stimulus of flicker received by the visual projection area of the cortex was breaking bounds—its ripples were overflowing into other areas."

Now, it is precisely this overflow of brain areas—hearing colors, seeing sounds, and even odors—that is a characteristic of the consciousness-expanding drugs. With flicker, Gray Walters produced many of the phenomena associated with consciousness-expanding drugs: "Subjects reported lights like comets, ultra-unearthly colors, mental colors, not deep visual ones." The literature of mescaline and LSD abounds in such regrettably vague descriptions of visionary experience.

Further experiments with subliminal doses of mescaline, accompanied by flicker-flicker administered under large doses, and repeated later—could well lead to a non-chemical method of expanding consciousness and increasing awareness. There are many consciousness-expanding drugs, each with distinct properties; and scientists are just beginning to explore the chemistry of these drugs. I have had personal experience with mescaline, LSD, bannisteria caapi, kava kava, dimethyl triptamine, and several others in the form of herbal preparations, the content of which was unknown to me. All of these drugs opened different psychic areas. Some of these areas are pleasant, some are not. Overdose of consciousness-expanding drugs can be a nightmare experience, owing to the increased awareness of unpleasant or dangerous symptoms. I would like to mention a drug which is neither a front-brain stimulant, like cocaine, nor a sedative, like morphine and a barbiturate; nor a tranquilizer, nor an energizer, nor a hallucinogen . . . a drug that acts as a useful stabilizing agent when using consciousness-expanding drugs.

This drug is apomorphine. I quote from "Anxiety and its Treatment," by Dr John Dent of London: "Apomorphine is made from morphine by boiling with hydrochloric acid, but its physiological effect is quite different. Apomorphine acts on the hypothalamus in such a way as to normalize metabolism and regulate the blood serum."

Administered with a consciousness-expanding drug, apomorphine stabilizes the experience and reduces anxiety. I have observed in others, and personally experienced, dramatic relief from anxiety resulting from consciousness-expanding drugs after a dose of apomorphine. This drug has no sedative or addicting qualities. No case of addiction to apomorphine has ever been recorded; yet, because of purely verbal association, the drug has been placed under the Harrison Narcotics Act, and is seldom prescribed in this country. Apomorphine is a unique drug, in that it acts as a metabolic regulator which stabilizes, but does not cancel the consciousness-expanding experience. In conclusion, the sedative drugs act to decrease awareness, and increased dosage is generally required to achieve or maintain this state of decreased awareness. The consciousness-expanding drugs act to increase awareness, and the state of increased awareness can be a permanent acquisition. It is unfortunate that cannabis, which is certainly one of the safest of the hallucinogenic drugs, should be subject to the heaviest legal sanctions. Unquestionably, this drug is very useful for the artist, activating trains of associations that would otherwise be inaccessible; and I owe many of the scenes in *Naked Lunch* directly to the use of cannabis. Opiates, on the other hand, since they have the effect of diminishing awareness of surroundings and bodily processes, can only be a hindrance to the artist. Cannabis serves as a guide to psychic areas which can then be re-entered without it. I have now discontinued the use of cannabis for some years, and I find that I am able to achieve the same results by non-chemical means: flicker and music through headphones, cut-ups and fold-ins of my texts, and especially by training myself to think in association blocks, instead of in words. That is, cannabis, like all the hallucinogens, can be discontinued, once the artist has familiarized himself with the areas opened by the drug. Cannabis sometimes causes anxiety, in large doses, and this anxiety is promptly relieved by apomorphine. It would seem to me that cannabis and the other hallucinogens provide a key to the creative process, and that a systematic study of these drugs would open the way to non-chemical methods of expanding consciousness.

Q : *Can it be said that, for our "alcoholic" Western nations, hallucinogens represent more of a danger for their system than as an actual physical threat, as we are led to believe?*

A : The official opposition to drugs is, as I have indicated in the last question, ambiguous: they condemn drugs as a danger to authority, but are drugs a real danger to the state? How dangerous is the tripper? Idle, perhaps, but the state is not in need of workers; on the contrary. Are trippers riot material? I suggest that the official opposition to drugs is a sham, that all the policies of the American Narcotics Department—and other countries who follow these policies, as England now is slavishly following the bad example of America, like a latter-day banana republic—are deliberately designed to spread the use of drugs, and the consequent unwise laws against the use of drugs.

Thus youth is deliberately led into these dead-end channels which are then made criminal by act of Congress or Parliament. This elementary chess move puts potential opposition in a concentration camp of criminality, weakened by the effects of such murderous drugs as methedrine—(there is absolutely no excuse for the manufacture of any variation of the benzedrine formula)—lulled into unwholesome states of love and oneness with the all and acceptance of everything by LSD, hooked on heroin, which, when illegal, takes up all the addict's time and makes him quite harmless. In short, drugs are an excellent method of state control; but this can never be uncovered by legalization, which they will fight all the way.

Russia, on the other hand, seems to take a more realistic view. The reason they oppose the use of cannabis is not because they think it is harmful, but because it makes a country more difficult to industrialize.

Both the physical and social dangers of drug use have been hopelessly confused by the systematic misinformation put out by the press...lurid stupid lies. They say that morphine addicts die within a few years. This is absurd. A morphine addict can live to be ninety. I know of one who did. Their general health is excellent. Heroin is more deteriorating than morphine, but does not have any immediate lethal results, if dosage is kept within reasonable limits, and if its use is not accompanied by the use of cocaine.

The press says that cannabis is habit-forming. It is not habit-forming, and no ill effects resulting from its use have ever been established. In countries where its use is widespread people smoke it all their lives without any demonstrable ill effects, except those resulting from the tobacco with which it is mixed. On the other hand, cocaine, methedrine, and all variations of the benzedrine formula, are ruinous to the health, even more so than alcohol.

The drug problem is camouflaged and like all problems wouldn't be there if things had been handled right in the beginning, considering a model drug problem in the United States where the addict is a criminal by legal definition and the proliferation of state laws making it a felony illegally to sell, possess or be addicted to opiates, marijuana, barbiturates, benzedrine, LSD and new drugs constantly added to the list. A continual outcry in the press creates interest and curiosity—people wanting to try these drugs, so more users more outcry more laws more young people in jail. Until even senators ask themselves plaintively

"Do we really want to put a good percentage of our young people in jail?"

"Is this our only answer to the narcotic problem?"

The American Narcotics Department says frankly yes, the drug user is a criminal and should be treated as such, jails, best cure for addicts. Experts say the laws must reflect society's disapproval of the addict. Possessing a reefer cigarette in the State of Texas you will see fifteen years of society's disapproval reflected from decent churchgoing eyes. Any serious attempt to actually enforce this welter of state and federal laws would entail a computerized invasion of privacy, a total police terror, a police machine that would pull the entire population into its orbit of violators, police, custody, courts, defense, probation and parole. Just tell the machine to enforce all laws by whatever means and the machine will sweep us to the disaster of a computerized police state.

Cannabis is certainly the safest of the hallucinogenic drugs in common use, large numbers of people in African and Near Eastern countries smoke it all their lives without apparent ill effects. As to its legalization in Western countries I do not have an opinion. If English doctors are empowered to prescribe heroin and cocaine it seems reasonable that they should also be empowered to prescribe cannabis. The stronger hallucinogenic drugs: LSD, mescaline, psylocybin, dim-N, bannisteria caapi, do present more serious dangers than their evangelical partisans would care to admit. States of panic are not infrequent and death has resulted from a "safe" dose of LSD. Recollect when I was traveling in the Putumayo town of Macoa laid up there a week with fever, stumbled on the story, man down from Cali if my memory serves, serious young student believed in telepathy read Lorca wanted to experience the "soul vine" bannisteria caapi, the Indians thereabouts call it "Yage," so the *brujo* brewed up his *brujo* dose he took himself man and boy forty years and passed it to the unfortunate traveler: one scream of hideous pain he rushed out into the jungle. They found him in a little clearing he was clearing with his convulsions. No charges were brought against the *brujo*, city feller got what he asked for. This sugary evil old man lived on to poison me some years later. However, mindful of the fate of my predecessor, I had provided myself with six nembutal capsules and twenty codeine tablets a piece of foresight to which I may well owe my life. Even so I lay on the ground outside the *brujo*'s hut for hours paralyzed in a hermetic vise of pain and fear. A high tolerance is acquired with use and the *brujo*'s daily dose to get his power up could readily be lethal to a novice.

Setting aside the factor of tolerance, there is considerable variation in reaction to these drugs from one individual to another a safe dose for one tripper could be dangerous for another. The prolonged use of LSD may give rise in some cases to a crazed unwholesome benevolence—the old tripster smiling into your face sees all your thoughts loving and accepting you inside out. Admittedly these drugs can be dangerous and they can give rise to deplorable states of mind.

To bring the use of these drugs into perspective I would suggest that academies be established where young people will learn to get really high...high as the Zen master is high when his arrow hits a target in the dark ...high as the karate master is high when he smashes a brick with his fist. . .high. . .weightless. . .in space. This is the space age. Time to look beyond this rundown radioactive cop-rotten planet. Time to look beyond this animal body. Remember anything that can be done chemically can be done in other ways. You don't need drugs to get high but drugs do serve as a useful short cut at certain stages of the training. The students would receive a basic course of training in the non-chemical discipline of Yoga, karate, prolonged sense withdrawal, stroboscopic lights, the constant use of tape recorders to break down verbal association lines. Techniques now being used for control of thought could be used instead for liberation. With computerized tape recorders and sensitive throat microphones we could attain insight into the nature of human speech and turn the word into a useful tool instead of an instrument of control in the hands of a misinformed and misinforming press.

Verbal techniques are now being used to achieve more reliable computer-processed techniques in the direction of opinion control and manipulation the "propaganda war" it's called. The CIA does not give away money for nothing. It gives away money for opinion control in certain directions. Opinion control is a technical operation extending over a period of years. First a population segment—"segment preparation"—is conditioned to react to words rather than word referents. You will notice in the subsidized periodicals a curious prose without image. If I say the word "chair" you see a chair. If I say "the concomitant somnolence with the ambivalent smugness of unavowed totalitarianism" you see nothing. This is pure word-conditioning the reader to react to words. "Preparations" so conditioned will then react predictably to words. The conditioned "preparation" is quite impervious to facts.

The aim of academy training is precisely *decontrol* of opinion, the students being conditioned to *look* at the facts *before* formulating any verbal patterns. The initial training in non-chemical methods of expanding awareness would last at least two years. During this period the student would be requested to refrain from all drugs including alcohol since bodily health is essential to minimize mental disturbance. After basic training the student would be prepared for drug trips to reach areas difficult to explore by other means in the present state of our knowledge.

The program proposed is essentially a disintoxication from inner fear and inner control, a liberation of thought and energy to prepare a new generation for the adventure of space. With such possibilities open to them I doubt if many young people would want the destructive drugs. Remember junk keeps you right here in junky flesh on this earth where Boot's is open all night. You can't make space in an aqualung of junk.

The problem of those already addicted remains. Addicts need medical treatment no jail and not prayers. I have spoken frequently of the apomorphine treatment as the quickest and most efficacious method of treating addicts. Variations and synthesis of the apomorphine formula might well yield a miracle drug for disintoxication. The drug lomotil, which greatly reduces the need for opiates, but is not in itself addicting, might prove useful. With experimentation a painless cure could certainly emerge. What makes a cure stick is when the cured addict finds something better to do and realizes he could not do it on junk. Academies of the type described would give young people something better to do incidentally reducing the drug problem to unimportance.

Q : Your answer to the last question would seem to imply that you consider anti-drug legislation more of a danger than drugs. Is this in point of fact your opinion?

A : Emphatically it is. What would happen if these drug laws were actually enforced to the letter? What would happen if *all* laws were actually enforced to the letter?

Enforce the law to the letter: . . . All the laws in these United States of America: . . . Arrest all violators of any law as set forth in all your books: . . . Arrest all violators regardless of race, color, creed, wealth or position. . .

"Thing Police made us. Joe get going."

Harry Bowers, 52, owned and managed a hotel. He was a good businessman who kept his books in perfect order. It was a hot June day in St. Louis day like any other breakfast at the Waldorf Cafeteria bacon eggs toast and coffee he was about to go back for another coffee when three accountant cops with narrow shoulders cold sulphurous grey eyes and bad teeth sat down at his table.

Brad and Greg were careful crewcut queers and they worked in a government office oh nothing secret just education they had a tasteful apartment in Georgetown just like Hempstead you know they had lived together fifteen years and it was mostly just platonic now and they were both tactful about each other's trade when they took their vacation in Tangier nothing local of course they'd decided that a long time ago and no gay bars they had responsible jobs they told each other well on this particular night after three Martinis and a beef ragout cooked by Greg who did the cooking while Brad cleaned up they had a rotation schedule of course they'd talked a lot about their relationship and decided one had to take a realistic view and arrange their life together day by day "our day" they called it according to a prearranged plan to avoid interpersonal friction during the working year when tempers frayed under the local trade ban that night after dinner and Brad hadn't had the two more too many looking through a new muscle magazine.

"That's *me!*"

"And my God that's *me!*"

They adjourned to the seeming privacy of their bedroom.

Jerry Wentworth was a cool pot smoker with a job in an ad agency. He had a cool soundproof pad with hi-fi and a slim model for his presence not sticking my neck out to legalize it rather have it my job and my apartment. Well one night right in the middle of Green Onions

"Hello Harry. I'm Joe." The agent showed a badge. "Yes Harry we work for that crazy American government. Buy you another coffee Harry?" The agent showed his dead grey teeth "Now I'm Joe Rogers of Internal Revenue and pleased to make your acquaintance I don't mind tell-

ing you some of the nicest people are violators. . .bar
furniture you sold off the books when you closed down
the bar after the war. . .poker game at Marty's. . .
pretty good poker player aren't you Harry? . . . day at the
races. . .it mounts up over the years." The agent slapped
a notebook on the table and stopped smiling. "Over the
past thirty years, Harry, better than ten thousand unde-
clared dollars crawled under your lying books." Coldly
the agents shoved their coffee checks at Harry Bowers.

Floodlights hit them in a silver blast: "What are you
doing in front of decent people?"

The door burst open and six Notre Dame fullback
agents shouldered into his cool pad flashing badges and
search warrants. An agent held up a joint. "You're cool
for twenty years dope freak."

The enforcement of existing laws inspired the salons.
The states vied with each other and Washington to pass
stricter laws. . .nutmeg. . .dandelions. . .unlicensed herb
gardens. . .narcotics as yet unclassified. . .penalties retroactive. . . permanent probation for second offenders.

Probation was computerized the "probs" being under
constant observation through television screens set up in
the places they were allowed to frequent. A second off-
screen and the machine spits out a warrant.

"So don't any of you 'probs' get ideas about a glass of
beer or something remember we got our screens every
place you could want to go if you think straight and
decent and we got our screens along the straightest route
between places. So learn your maze and stay on screen."

Since police activity was largely directed toward narcotics, tax chiselers, obscenity and sex offenses and since
no citizen in his senses would go near a police station
crimes against person and property flourished with virtual
impunity and many old-fashioned criminals rose through
fink ranks to high police positions. The citizen, stagger-
ing under escalating taxes, set upon by brazen muggers,

searched and questioned by the police at every street corner, crept back to his burglarized apartment.

The space program was forgotten. National defense was neglected in favor of "the great American task."

"What would happen if this country were attacked?" Senator Bradly demanded. "Ninety per cent of the eighteen to twenty-five-year-olds are in jail and the remaining ten per cent is on the cops."

He was denounced in the press as "a bleeding heart, the advocate of pansies, criminals, and dope freaks."

The overloaded machine is breaking down. Mistakes are now pandemic. The innocent householder shivers knowing that his sugar may well assay 100 per cent heroin. Citizens reporting to pay a parking ticket are bustled into the death cell as the berserk machine spits out random laws, warrants and sentences. The number of internees swells ominously...ten million, twenty million, forty million.

America is a shell around an explosive core of sullen prisoners. Senator Bradly rises for the last time to say "God help us all!"

The American Moral Disease spreads to other countries. Police fear darkens the earth. In 1959 I wrote: "Infection dedicated to traffic in exchange narcotics demonstrated a Typhoid Mary who will spread the narcotics problem to the United Kingdom" ... *Nova Express*... Jonathan Cape, page 60... That same year doctor John Dent met a doctor from the American Narcotics Department. The narco doctor told him: "I have a hunch you English will have our narcotics problem in ten years time."

London 1969: Everywhere the pot-sniffing fink hounds now trained to smell out LSD, cocaine, heroin, opium, pep pills, and purple hearts. Dogs at the airport sniffing the tourists' dogs in the bank smelling checks nuzzling an old man's groin in the East India Club opening handbags in Fortnum's Fountain with their teeth police with dogs seal off any block at both ends and the citizen is required to stand with his coat open while a dog snuffles him over from head to foot so back to his unheated apartment—(widespread power cuts you know)—a police-woman in the medicine cabinet again wants to know if he would care to explain this rectal syringe. A forensic chemist states flatly: "Speaking for all the kids in lab we are tired of having ashes, garbage, dustbins, clothes, drapes, rugs, vacuum cleaner bags and water dipped from toilet bowls dumped into the forensic laboratories. We've got warehouses full of this muck now and it will take us years to process it." Sullen muttering flares to open revolt. An infuriated mob storms the Home Office screaming: "DEATH TO THE FINK DOGS!"

In Hyde Park six dogs are torn from a policewoman's lead, doused with gasoline and burned to death before a vast cheering crowd. Demolition squads are attacking the American machine. In South America and Africa guerrilla units call on violators of all nations to join them in armies of liberation. "We will march on the police machine and destroy it everywhere. We will destroy all its records. We will destroy the house organ of the police machine that goes under the name of conservative press."

All from an old movie will give at their touch.

Q : Are the effects of drugs worse than those of alcohol?

A : Alcohol sedates the front brain relieving anxiety and discontent and is certainly a factor in preserving the *status quo* in Western countries. Of all drugs in common use, alcohol has the worst statistic as regards damage physical mental and moral to the individual and to society. How many crimes are committed every day by people under the influence of alcohol, crimes *directly* traceable to alcohol, crimes that would not have been committed had the person been sober? Drunken fights, drunken murders, drunken car accidents. How much objectionable, stupid, boring behavior is due to alcohol? How many people are degraded by its use? How much money and time is spent on alcohol? How much inefficiency is caused by its use or by the after-effects of its use? And how many illnesses can be directly attributed to alcohol? Cirrhosis of the liver, kidney disease, alcoholism, Korsokov's psychosis, stomach ulcers. How anyone can oppose legalization of cannabis without at the same time being an ardent prohibitionist is beyond my understanding.

Q : *Addiction is a prison. Is domination by drugs comparable to domination by the images and myths created by our civilization? Is it worse?*

A : It is very dangerous to use the word "addiction" loosely, as addiction to images, myths, etc., though this can occur. Addiction means something that causes acute physical and mental discomfort if it is withdrawn. Perhaps the closest parallel is what I might call an addiction to rightness, to being in the right; such an addict—and their name is legion—experiences acute discomfort if his rightness is withdrawn. Without it he is nothing, and he cannot adjust to normal metabolism—that is, the realization that rightness and wrongness are relative concepts that have meaning only relative to position and purpose. I recall a French fascist who said: "Je ne comprends pas ces degeneres de la drogue comme William Burroughs."—(I wasn't on drugs at the time.)—"Moi, j'ai une seule drogue. C'est l'indignation." C'est la pire...it's the worst drug of all.

Q : *How did you get involved with drugs?*

A : Addiction is an illness of exposure. I was associated with addicts and since morphine was available to me I took it from time to time and eventually became addicted.

Q : *Have many addicts successfully withdrawn from junk by the conventional methods? Have you tried them?*

A : Very few addicts are successfully withdrawn by conventional methods because the physiological need remains like the head of a tapeworm. I have tried them all slow withdrawals, quick withdrawals, prolonged sleep, cortisone, antihistamines. None of them work.

Q : What does the discovery of apomorphine represent in your life?

A : The turning point between life and death. I would never have been cured without it. *Naked Lunch* would never have been written.

ANTI-JUNK

Addiction is a metabolic illness and no more a police problem than tuberculosis or radium poisoning. The American Narcotics Department has persisted in regarding addiction as criminal in itself with the consequent emphasis on punishment rather than treatment. We're told that the laws against addiction must reflect society's disapproval of the addict—that is to say, cause society's disapproval of the addict. Recently when an attempt was made to set up a treatment center in Hoboken, the local inhabitants stoned the center screaming, "Are you high?" "Did you bring your needle?" "We will never accept criminal men and women in Hoboken!"

When I was in high school in the 1920's the use of any drug other than alcohol was unknown. When I first became addicted to heroin in the 1940's teen-age addicts were still unknown. Now the rising incidence of teen-age addiction has led to extending control measures that have yielded lamentable results.

Addiction is an illness of exposure. The stringent measures of the American Narcotics Department, their vociferous insistence that addiction is a police and not a medical problem, spread the infection among young people.

In the 1920's and 30's heroin was much more readily available than it is now to those already addicted. Pushers sold to addicts, and most of their business came from the seedy furtive smalltime underworld, shortchange artists, thieves, pimps and whores. It was a world of shabby streets and rooming houses far removed from high school students. At that time it was quite easy to support a morphine habit from doctor's prescriptions, and many of the old itinerant con men used this route exclusively. When the American Narcotics Department, berserk with Parkinson's Law, began a program of wholesale arrest and disproportionate sentences for possession, many of the old-time addicts and pushers were put out of circulation . . . Some old-timers quit in disgust. Even the Mafia decided there are safer and easier ways to make money.

As a result, a whole new generation of users and pushers arose. This new generation of pushers turned to the teenage market. This development was easy to foresee by any person with a clear mind. Am I saying that the American Narcotics Department *deliberately* spread the illness of addiction to young people? Whether an agent acts deliberately or not is about as interesting as how many angels can dance on the point of a pin. By their fruits you will know them, and the fruits of the American Narcotics Department are deplorable.

This brings us to the possibility of quarantining or containing the illness of addiction, which has been the English system. In England a doctor may prescribe any amount of heroin for an addicted patient, but will not prescribe unless he has satisfied himself the patient is already addicted. Since heroin is available to an addict legally and he can buy it at drugstore prices, he does not need to buy on the black market—though admittedly an addict may sell off a pill or two from his allowance to other addicts in the United States. Recently pressure from American sources has been brought to bear on England and there is talk of changing the system. English doctors are opposed to the change, since they feel it will give police officers the right to tell a doctor what he can and cannot prescribe.

This right has long been vested in the American Narcotics Department and a doctor may lose his license if he prescribes for addicts. The pretext of looking for narcotics gives them the right to search any person or premises at any time. The Department is continually lobbying for more anti-narcotic laws and stiffer penalties. Many of the laws passed under this pressure are very dangerous indeed to our so-called freedom. In Louisiana and California it is a felony to be an addict. Penalizing a state of being, apart from any proven illegal act, sets a precedent that could be extended to other categories of "offenders," including anyone opposed to official policies. To classify all opposition as criminal is of course the simple device by which a fascist regime takes over and proclaims a majority.

In December, 1964, I returned to the States and was detained three hours at customs while narcotics agents read my notes, letters and diary. Finding no narcotics, they then informed me I was subject to fine and imprisonment for failing to register with the Department when I left the country, and for failing to inform the customs officer of my narcotics record on my return. The law requiring addicts to register only applies to those who have been convicted under federal, state or city violations of the Harrison Narcotics Act or the Marijuana Act of 1937. I have been arrested twice in the United States, once 17 years ago and once 20 years ago. In neither case was I convicted. In any case, this law would seem to make it a crime ever to have been an addict.

And what does the Treatment Center at Lexington, Kentucky, offer? A ten-day reduction cure with methadone, yielding almost unanimous relapse at the first opportunity, as the doctors at Lexington readily admit. The head of the research department at Lexington is Dr Isbell. Dr Dent, founder of *The English Society for the Study of Addictions*, was never able to interest him in the apomorphine treatment he had pioneered and used successfully for 40 years. I know of one occasion when Dr Isbell talked with two of Dr Dent's cured patients.

He told Dr Dent that he considered the treatment "too dangerous." Dangerous to whom? Experiments at Lexington seem oriented toward establishing the addictive liability of decorticated canine preparations! Yes, even a dog with its brains cut out can be hooked. I could have told you that before you stuck the needle in, doc.

The treatment at Lexington is now six months of confinement after the initial ten-day reduction with substitute drugs. Public Health officials now wish to extend this period, saying that prolonged involuntary confinement is necessary because the addict does not "want" to be cured. Of course addicts do not "want" to be cured, since it is precisely the centers of "wanting" that have been taken over by the drug. When they begin to lose the need for morphine in the course of the apomorphine treatment, many will "want" to continue the treatment and stay off drugs. The apomorphine treatment takes about eight to ten days. After treatment the cured addict finds that he can resist relapse. Apomorphine precisely activates the resistance centers.

If the official agencies have failed to solve the narcotics problem to state it honestly, the nonofficial agencies have done little better. Recently, centers of treatment have sprung up where the addicts receive no other medication than prayer. This inspirational and quasi-religious approach to a metabolic illness is ill-advised. It would be equally logical to prescribe prayer for malaria. Recently in New York, doctors have been allowed to prescribe methadone for heroin addiction. Addicts lose the desire for heroin in the course of this treatment. Over a period of five years they hope to reduce the dosage of methadone. Methadone is an opiate stronger than morphine and quite as addictive. To say that addicts have been cured of heroin by the use of methadone is like saying an alcoholic has been cured of whisky by the use of gin. If the addicts lose their desire for heroin it is because the methadone dosage is stronger than the diluted heroin they receive from pushers.

Junk is a generic term for all habit-forming preparations and derivatives of opium including the synthetics. There are also non-habit forming derivatives and preparations of opium. Papaverene, which is found in raw opium, is non-habit forming. Apomorphine, which is derived from morphine, is non-habit forming. Yet both substances are classified as narcotics in America under the Harrison Narcotics Act.

Any form of junk can cause addiction. Nor does it make much difference whether it is injected, sniffed or taken orally. The result is always the same—addiction. The addict functions on junk. Like a diver depends on his air line, the addict depends on his junk line. When his junk is cut off, he suffers agonizing withdrawal symptoms: watering burning eyes, light fever, hot and cold flashes, leg and stomach cramps, diarrhea, insomnia, prostration, and in some cases death from circulatory collapse and shock. Withdrawal symptoms are distinguished from any syndrome of comparable severity by the fact that they are immediately relieved by administering a sufficient quantity of opiates. The withdrawal symptoms reach their peak on the fourth day, then gradually disappear over a period of three to six weeks. The later stages of withdrawal are marked by profound depression.

The time necessary to establish addiction varies with individual susceptibility and the addictive strength of the preparation used. Normally, anyone who receives daily injections totalling one grain of morphine every day for a month will experience considerable discomfort if the injections are discontinued. Four to six months of use is enough to establish full addiction. By and large, those become addicts who have access to junk. In Iran, where opium was sold openly in shops, they had three million addicts. There is no more a pre-addict personality than there is a pre-malarial personality, all the hogwash of psychiatry to the contrary. (It is my opinion that nine out of ten psychiatrists should be broken down to veterinarians and their books called in for pulping.) To say it country simple, most folks enjoy junk. Having once experienced this pleasure the human organism will tend to repeat it and repeat it and repeat it. The addict's illness is junk. Knock on any door. Whatever answers the door, give it four half-grain shots of God's Own Medicine every day for six months and the so-called "addict personality" is there. . .an old junky selling Christmas Seals on North Clark Street, the "Priest" they called him, seedy and furtive cold fish eyes that seem to be looking at something other folks can't see. That something he is looking at is junk.

The whole addict personality can be summed up in one sentence: the addict needs junk. He will do a lot to get junk just as you would do a lot for water if you were thirsty enough. You see, junk is a personality—a seedy grey man couldn't be anything else but junk rooming-house a shabby street room on the top floor these stairs cough the "Priest" there pulling himself up along the banister bathroom yellow wood panels dripping toilet works stacked under the washbasin back in his room now cooking up grey shadow on a distant wall used to be me Mister. I was on junk for almost 15 years. In that time I took ten cures. I have been to Lexington: the day after I got out, dressed in my banker suit and carrying *The Wall Street Journal*: buying paregoric "It's my wife she uh. . ."

"I quite understand sir. Would you like the two-ounce family size?"

"Why yes I believe so."

I have taken abrupt withdrawal treatments and prolonged withdrawal treatments, cortisone, tranquilizers, antihistamines and the prolonged sleep cure. In every case I relapsed at the first opportunity. Why do addicts voluntarily take a cure and then relapse? I think on a deep biological level most addicts want to be cured. Junk is death and your body knows it. I relapsed because I was never physiologically cured until I took the apomorphine treatment. Apomorphine is the only agent I know that evicts the "addict personality," my old friend Opium Jones. We were mighty close in Tangier, 1957, shooting every hour 15 grains of methadone per day which equals 30 grains of morphine and that's a lot of GOM. I never changed my clothes. Jones likes his clothes to season in stale rooming-house flesh until you can tell by a hat on the table a coat hung over a chair that Jones lives there. I never took a bath. Old Jones don't like the feel of water on his skin. I spent whole days looking at the end of my shoe just communing with Jones. Then one day I saw that Jones was not a real friend that our interests were in fact divergent. So I took a plane to London and found Dr Dent charcoal fire in the grate Scottish terrier cup of tea. He told me about the treatment and I entered the nursing home the following day. It was one of those four-story buildings on Cromwell Road room with rose wallpaper on the third floor. I had a day nurse and a night nurse and received an injection of apomorphine 1/20th grain every two hours day and night. Dr Dent told me I could have morphine if I needed it but the amount would be small, 1/12th what I had been using, with quite a cut again the next day.

Now every addict has his special symptom, the one that hits him hardest when his junk is cut off. With me it's *feeling* the slow painful death of Mr Jones. Listen to the old-timers in Lexington talking about their symptoms:

"Now with me it's puking is the worst."

"I never puke. It's this cold burn on my skin drives me up the wall."

"My trouble is sneezing."

"I feel myself encased in the old grey corpse of Mr

Jones. Not another person in this world I want to see. Not a thing I want to do except revive Mr Jones."

Third day cup of tea at dawn calm miracle of apomorphine I was learning to live without Jones, reading newspapers writing letters, most cases I can't write a letter for a month and here I was writing a letter on the third day and looking forward to a talk with Dr Dent who isn't Jones at all. Apomorphine had taken care of my special symptom. Seven days after entering the nursing home I got my last 8-grain shot. Three days later I left the hospital. I went back to Tangier where junk was readily available at that time. I didn't have to use will power, whatever that is. I just didn't want any junk. The apomorphine treatment had given me a long calm look at all the grey junk yesterdays, a long calm look at Mr Jones standing there in his shabby black suit and grey felt hat stale rooming-house flesh cold undersea eyes. So I boiled him in hydrochloric acid. Only way to get him clean you understand layers and layers of that grey junk rooming-house smell.

Apomorphine is made from morphine by boiling with hydrochloric acid, but its physiological action is quite different. Morphine sedates the front brain. Apomorphine stimulates the back brain and the vomiting centers. 1/12th grain of apomorphine injected will produce vomiting in a few minutes, and for many years the only use made of this drug was as an emetic in cases of poisoning.

When Dr Dent started using the apomorphine treatment, 40 years ago, all his patients were alcoholics. He would put a bottle of whisky by the bed and invite the patient to drink all he wanted. But with each drink the patient received an injection of apomorphine. After a few days the patient conceived such a distaste for alcohol that he would ask to have the bottle removed from the room. Dr Dent thought at first that this was due to a conditioned aversion, since the spirit was associated with a dose of apomorphine that often produced vomiting. However, he found that some of his patients were not in the least nauseated by the dose of apomorphine received. Nonetheless these patients experienced the same distaste for alcohol and voluntarily stopped drinking after a few days of treatment. He concluded that his patients conceived a distaste for alcohol because they no longer needed it and that apomorphine acts on the back brain to regulate metabolism, so that the body no longer needs a sedative to which it had become accustomed. From that time he stressed the fact that apomorphine is a metabolic regulator, and it is the only drug known that acts in this way to normalize a disturbed metabolism. *Apomorphine is not an aversion treatment.*

If a program is properly presented many addicts will report voluntarily for treatment. Those who volunteer for treatment are the best prospects and will provide an ever-increasing number of testimonials to its success. If the addict is informed that he will get junk if he needs it, he will be much more willing to undergo treatment. At the end of a month patients could be discharged and given a prescription for oral apomorphine tablets to use in case of relapse. Apomorphine is completely non-habit forming and no case of addiction to apomorphine has ever been recorded.

Like a good policeman, apomorphine does its work and goes. The fact that it is not an addictive substitute drug is crucial. In any reduction cure the addict knows that he is still receiving narcotics, and he dreads the time when the last dose is withdrawn. In the apomorphine treatment the addict knows he is getting better without morphine.

I feel that any form of so-called psychotherapy is strongly contra-indicated for addicts. Addicts should not be led to dwell on or relive the addict experience since this conduces to relapse. The question, "Why did you start using narcotics in the first place?" should never be asked. It is quite as irrelevant to treatment as it would be to ask a malarial patient why he went to a malarial area.

Apomorphine has proven useful in the treatment of other addictions and chronic intoxications. There are thousands of barbiturate addicts in the United States, and the treatment of this addiction is even more difficult and time-consuming than the treatment of heroin addiction. The withdrawal of barbiturates must be effected very slowly and under constant supervision. Otherwise the addict is subject to convulsive seizures that can result in serious injuries. Barbiturate addicts treated with apomorphine can be cut off barbiturates immediately without convulsions or other serious symptoms. Barbiturate addicts suffer from severe insomnia during withdrawal and it may be some weeks before the sleep cycle is normalized. Treated with apomorphine they sleep normally. Amphetamine users, on the other hand, often fall into such a deep sleep when the drug is cut off that they cannot be aroused to eat. Treated with apomorphine they sleep normally and can be easily aroused. This brings us once again to the unique value of apomorphine as a drug that normalizes metabolism, which would indicate its use in conditions other than addiction.

Dr Feldman of Switzerland has noted that in cases showing an excess of cholesterol in the blood this condition disappeared after treatment with apomorphine. Dr Xavier Coor of Paris told me recently that he finds apomorphine an extremely useful drug in general practice. He prescribes apomorphine for anxiety, grief, nervousness, insomnia—in short, for all the conditions where tranquilizers and barbiturates are usually given. Certainly it is a much safer drug since there is no danger of addiction or even dependence. When you take apomorphine for a severe emotional state you have faced the problem, not avoided it. The apomorphine has normalized your metabolism, always disturbed in any emotional upset, so that you can face the problem with calmness and sanity.

Apomorphine is listed as a narcotic in the United States, and subject to the same regulations as morphine and heroin with regard to prescription and use. In both France and England apomorphine is not on the dangerous drug list. A doctor's prescription is required but the prescription can be refilled any number of times. It is difficult to avoid the conclusion that a deliberate attempt has been made in the United States to mislead medical opinion and minimize the value of the apomorphine treatment.

No variation of the apomorphine formula has ever been manufactured and the formula has never been synthesized. With synthesis and variation the side effect of vomiting could probably be eliminated, and drugs developed exerting ten or fifty times the regulatory action of the existing preparation. These drugs could excise from the planet what we call anxiety. Since all monopolistic and hierarchical systems are basically rooted in anxiety, it is not surprising that the use of the apomorphine treatment or the synthesis of the apomorphine formula have been consistently opposed in certain drearily predictable quarters.

Q : *How did you come to be introduced to this antidote?*

A : I had been referred by my doctor in Palm Beach to an English doctor who in turn referred me to Doctor Dent.

Q : *Have you undergone apomorphine treatment several times?*

A : Yes. The treatment does not ensure that no relapse will occur. It makes a relapse less likely to occur. Relapse with conventional treatment is almost inevitable.

Apomorphine can head off a relapse. If an addict has taken a few shots prompt administration of apomorphine can avert a complete relapse.

Q : *How does it happen that such an apparently effective cure is not in more general use?*

A : The American Medical Association and the American
Narcotics Department have consistently opposed its use.
Since writing this article I have received many letters from
addicts and alcoholics who desperately needed and wanted
help. I answered these letters. I quote from replies:

"At my request my family doctor has tried to find additional
information about the drug and the treatment in this country. Unfortunately we have had no success."

"The research I was about to undertake on Doctor Dent's
former patients has sadly for various reasons had to be called
off."

"The American Medical Association seems to be afraid of
this drug."

In short, people who desperately need this treatment are
not able to obtain it.

Q : *Your efforts to publicize apomorphine have been many.
What have been your relations with people who would be
competent to prescribe apomorphine in hospitals which
treat addicts?*

A : I have indeed received many letters from probation
agents and doctors engaged in the treatment and rehabili-
tation of addicts. In all cases so far the results have been
negative. Pressure has been brought to bear, some of them
have lost their jobs as a result. Dr Isbell, who is the research head at Lexington Narcotics Center for the U.S.
Government, says that apomorphine is "too dangerous."
Dangerous to whom, exactly? Dangerous to those who
wish addiction to continue unchecked by any effective
treatment, as an "insoluble problem."

Q : *Couldn't apomorphine be publicized by the press, which
is always after a scandal?*

A : No. The press is working with the Narcotics Department to publicize and spread the drug problem. It is not
to their interest to stop this source of copy and circulation

by advocating measures that would control drug addiction and reduce it to a minor health problem. What is the press selling? Violence, sex, and drugs. These items are sure copy. That is to say, effective measures to eliminate criminality or drug-taking are not good copy.

Q : What is the opinion of pharmaceutical researchers on the merit of apomorphine?

A : Pharmaceutical researchers are told what research to pursue by vested interest, which gives orders to the American Narcotics Department. Billions for variations on the benzedrine formula, for tranquilizers of dubious value, not ten cents for a drug that has unlimited potentials not only in treating addiction but in handling the whole problem of anxiety.

Q : If it were widely used, apomorphine might be a source of considerable income for pharmaceutical companies. Why doesn't this interest them?

A : They can sell all the products they produce in any case. Remember, these pharmaceutical companies have a vested interest in illness. Drugs that strike at the very root of illness are "dangerous."

Q : Is it because of financial interests that there is a blockade against apomorphine?

A : Financial and power interests. As I have pointed out, drugs are one of the most effective potential weapons against revolt from the 18–25-year-old age group.

Q : Does the state share the income from drug traffic? Is this one of the reasons for the silence surrounding apomorphine?

A : Only indirectly. The drug traffic gives work to thousands of agents and is a pretext for almost unlimited appropriations.

Q : Can apomorphine be used to treat other people besides addicts?

A : Definitely yes. Dr Xavier Coor of France states that he has found it one of the most useful drugs in general practice, being prescribed for insomnia, grief, nervousness, generalized anxiety—in short, for every condition for which tranquilizers are now prescribed. Apomorphine is not addictive nor does it produce any sort of habituation. No one would use it unless he needs it. It does its work and goes.

Q : Is addiction growing rapidly on the worldwide level?

A : Addiction is certainly growing throughout the Western world—that is, in areas where it was formerly confined to a relatively few cases. On the other hand, it has been eliminated in China. It is probably stationary in countries like India and Persia, where the use of opium has been endemic for hundreds of years, thousands perhaps.

Q : Is mescaline physiologically harmful?

A : Mescaline may well be dangerous: it's nauseating, and can cause acute anxiety and mental disturbance.

Q : Do you think that the use of certain hallucinogens could make the masses conscious of fundamental problems?

A : No. In countries where cannabis is legal or at least is used unopposed by the authorities, there is no evidence of any consciousness of fundamental problems. What would happen if cannabis were legal? Nothing special.

Q : Does turning on or tripping show you the truth, does it make human preoccupations seem foolish, reveal the comic vanity of power and possession?

A : These drugs may give insight into basic realities and the vanity of human pretensions. However, the insights may not be permanent, and in many cases they are distorted.

Q : In The Yage Letters, you describe the adventures which took you to Putamayo in the Upper Amazon in search of yage. Was the discovery important?

A : Yage is one of the most interesting of the hallucinogens, and very little research has been done.

Q : Have you written much under the influence of drugs? What results did you get? Can these results be compared with those that you get from cut-ups?

A : To put writing done under the influence of drugs into a special category is absurd. Writing is writing, good, bad, successful, unsuccessful. I have written a good deal under the influence of cannabis; many sections of *Naked Lunch* were so written. I have often heard it said that what is written under the influence of drugs seems to the writer of great worth at the time, whereas examined after the drug wears off it is pretentious nonsense. The same is true of any writing. I have frequently written without drugs a passage I thought was marvelous; reading it over the next day, into the wastebasket. On the other hand, passages written with cannabis have stood the test of critical after-inspection. Some have and some have not. I have attempted to write after taking mescaline, but was deterred by nausea and lack of physical coordination. On the other hand, after the drug had worn off I was able to describe the psychic areas revealed to me by the drug. Amphetamine and cocaine are quite worthless for writing and nothing of value remains. I have never been able to write a line under the influence of alcohol. Under morphine one can edit, type, and organize material effectively but since the drug acts to decrease awareness the creative factor is dimmed. *Junkie* is the only one of my books written under the influence of opiates. The other books could never have been written if I had been addicted to morphine at the time.

Q : What do you think of the texts which try to describe the visions offered by drugs?

A : For the most part dull. The writer has forgotten that he is a writer. He thinks that his vision is interesting in itself which it usually is not.

Q : Can the use of the tape recorder effectively replace that of drugs to break down the barriers of consciousness and enlarge the field of perceptions?

A : Yes. Tape recorder experiments such as I have described in the invisible generation do produce highs and do enlarge the field of perception. . .

THE INVISIBLE GENERATION

what we see is determined to a large extent by what we hear   you can verify this proposition by a simple experiment   turn off the sound track on your television set and substitute an arbitrary sound track prerecorded on your tape recorder street sounds music conversation recordings of other television programs   you will find that the arbitrary sound track seems to be appropriate and is in fact determining your interpretation of the film track on screen people running for a bus in piccadilly with a sound track of machine-gun fire looks like 1917 petrograd   you can extend the experiment by using recorded material more or less appropriate to the film track for example take a political speech on television shut off sound track and substitute another speech you have prerecorded   hardly tell the difference isn't much record sound track of one danger man from uncle spy program run it in place of another and see if your friends can't tell the difference   it's all done with tape recorders   consider this machine and what it can do   it can record and play back activating a past time set by precise association a recording can be played back any number of times you can study and analyze every pause and inflection of a recorded conversation why did so and so say just that or this just here play back so and so's recordings and you will find out what cues so and so in you can edit a recorded conversation retaining material which is incisive witty and pertinent   you can edit a recorded conversation retaining remarks which are boring flat and silly   a tape recorder can play back back fast   slow or backwards   you can learn to do these things   record a sentence and speed it up   now try imitating your accelerated voice   play a sentence backwards and learn to unsay what you just said... such exercises bring you a liberation from old association locks   try inching tape   this sound is produced by taking a recorded text for best results a text spoken in a loud clear voice and rubbing the tape back and forth across the head   the same sound can be produced on a philips compact cassette recorder by playing a tape back and switching the mike control stop start on and off at short intervals which gives an effect of stuttering   take any text speed it up slow it down run it backwards inch it and you will hear words that were not in the original recording new words made by the machine   different people will scan out different words of course but some of the words are quite clearly there and anyone can hear them words which were not in the original tape but which are in many cases relevant to the original text as if the words themselves had been interrogated and forced to reveal their hidden meanings it is interesting to record these words words literally made by the machine itself   you can carry this experiment further using as your original recording material that contains no words animal noises for instance record a trough of slopping hogs the barking of dogs   go to the zoo and record the bellowings of Guy the gorilla the big cats growling over their meat goats and monkeys   now run the animals backwards speed up slow down and inch the animals and see if any clear words emerge   see what the animals have to say see how the animals react to playback of processed tape the simplest variety of cut up on tape can be carried out with one machine like this record any text rewind to the beginning   now run forward at arbitrary intervals stop the machine and record a short text wind forward stop record where you have recorded over the original text the words are wiped out and replaced with new words   do this several times creating arbitrary juxtapositions   you will notice that the arbitrary cuts in are appropriate in many cases and your cut up tape makes surprising sense   cut up tapes can be hilariously funny twenty years ago i heard a tape called the drunken newscaster prepared by jerry newman of new york cutting up news broadcasts i can not remember the words at this distance but i do remember laughing until i fell out of a chair paul bowles calls the tape recorder god's little toy maybe his last toy fading into the cold spring air poses a colorless question

any number can play

yes any number can play   anyone with a tape recorder controlling the sound track   can influence and create events   the tape recorder experiments described here will show you how this influence can be extended and correlated into the precise operation   this is the invisible generation he looks like an advertising executive a college student an american tourist doesn't matter what your cover story is so long as it covers you and leaves you free to act you need a philips compact cassette recorder handy machine for street recording and playback   you can carry it under your coat for recording looks like a transistor radio for playback   playback in the street will show the influence of your sound track in operation of course the most undetectable playback is street recordings people don't notice yesterday voices phantom car holes in time accidents of past time played back in present time screech of brakes loud honk of an absent horn can occasion an accident here   old fires still catch old buildings still fall or take a prerecorded sound track into the street anything you want to put out on the sublim eire play back two minutes record two minutes mixing your message with the street   waft your message right into a worthy ear some carriers are much better than others you know the ones lips moving muttering away carry my message 'all over london in our yellow submarine working with street playback you will see your playback find the appropriate context for example i am playing back some of my dutch schultz last word tapes in the street five alarm fire and a fire truck passes right on cue   you will learn to give the cues you will learn to plant events and concepts   after analyzing recorded conversations you will learn to steer a conversation where you want it to go   the physiological liberation achieved as word lines of controlled association are cut will make you more efficient in reaching your objectives   whatever you do you will do it better   record your boss and co-workers analyze their associational patterns learn to imitate their voices oh you'll be a popular man around the office but not easy to compete with the usual procedure record their body sounds from concealed mikes the rhythm of breathing the movements of after-lunch intestines the beating of hearts now impose your own body sounds and become the breathing word and the beating heart of that organization   become that organization   the invisible brothers are invading present time   the more people we can get working with tape recorders the more useful experiments and extensions will turn up   why not give tape recorder parties every guest arrives with his recorder and tapes of what he intends to say at the party recording what other recorders say to him it is the height of rudeness not to record when addressed directly by another tape recorder and you can't say anything directly have to record it first the coolest old tape worms never talk direct

what was the party like   switch on playback
what happened at lunch   switch on playback
eyes old unbluffed unreadable he hasn't said a direct word in ten years and as you hear what the party was like

and what happened at lunch you will begin to see sharp
and clear there was a grey veil between you and what
you saw or more often did not see that grey veil was the
prerecorded words of a control machine once that veil is
removed you will see clearer and sharper than those who
are behind the veil whatever you do you will do it better
than those behind the veil this is the invisible generation it is the efficient generation hands work and go
see some interesting results when several hundred tape
recorders turn up at a political rally or a freedom
march suppose you record the ugliest snarling southern
law men several hundred tape recorders spitting it back
and forth and chewing it around like a cow with the
aftosa you now have a sound that could make any neighborhood unattractive several hundred tape recorders
echoing the readers could touch a poetry reading with
unpredictable magic and think what fifty thousand beatle
fans armed with tape recorders could do to shea sta-
dium several hundred people recording and playing
back in the street is quite a happening right there conservative m.p. spoke about the growing menace posed by
bands or irresponsible youths with tape recorders playing
back traffic sounds that confuse motorists carrying the
insults recorded in some low underground club into mayfair and piccadilly this growing menace to public order put a thousand young recorders with riot recordings
into the street that mutter gets louder and louder remember this is a technical operation one step at a time
here is an experiment that can be performed by anyone
equipped with two machines connected by extension lead
so he can record directly from one machine to the
other since the experiment may give rise to a marked
erotic reaction it is more interesting to select as your
partner some one with whom you are on intimate terms
we have two subjects b. and j. b. records on tape recorder 1 j. records on tape recorder 2 now we alternate
the two voice tracks tape recorder 1 playback two sec-

onds tape recorder 2 records   tape recorder 2 playback
two seconds tape recorder 1 records alternating the voice
of b. with the voice of j.   in order to attain any degree
of precision the two tapes should be cut with scissors and
alternate pieces spliced together   this is a long process
which can be appreciably expedited if you have access to
a cutting room and use film tape which is much larger and
easier to handle   you can carry this experiment further
by taking a talking film of b. and talking film of j. splicing
sound and image track twenty four alternations per second   as i have intimated it is advisable to exercise some
care in choosing your partner for such experiments since
the results can be quite drastic b. finds himself talking and
thinking just like j.   j. sees b.'s image in his own face
who's face   b. and j. are continually aware of each
other   when separated invisible and persistent presence
they are in fact becoming each other   you see b. retroactively was j. by the fact of being recorded on j.'s sound
and image track experiments with spliced tape can give
rise to explosive relationships properly handled of course
to a high degree of efficient cooperation you will begin
to see the advantage conveyed on j. if he carried out such
experiments without the awareness of b. and so many
applications of the spliced tape principle will suggest
themselves to the alert reader suppose you are some creep
in a grey flannel suit you want to present a new concept
of advertising to the old man it is creative advertising so
before you goes up against the old man you record the
old man's voice and splices your own voice in expounding
your new concept and put it out on the office air-condi-
tioning system splice yourself in with your favorite pop
singers   splice yourself in with newscasters prime minis-
ters presidents

why stop there

why stop anywhere

everybody splice himself in with everybody else yes
boys that's me there by the cement mixer   the next step

and i warn you it will be expensive is programmed tape
recorders   a fully programmed machine would be set to
record and play back at selected intervals to rewind and
start over after a selected interval automatically remaining in continuous operation   suppose you have three
programmed machines tape recorder 1 programmed to play
back five seconds while tape recorder 2 records   tape
recorder 2 play back three seconds while tape recorder 1
records now say you are arguing with your boy friend or
girl friend remembering what was said last time and
thinking of things to say next time round and round you
just can't shut up   put all your arguments and com-
plaints on tape recorder 1 and call tape recorder 1 by
your own name   on tape recorder 2 put all the things he
or she said to you or might say when occasion arises out
of the tape recorders   now make the machines talk   tape
recorder 1 play back five seconds tape recorder 2 record   tape recorder 2 play back three seconds tape recorder 1 record   run it through fifteen minutes half an
hour   now switch intervals running the interval switch
you used on tape recorder 1 back on tape recorder 2   the
interval switch may be as important as the context   listen
to the machines mix it around   now on tape recorder
3 you can introduce the factor of irrelevant response so put
just anything on tape recorder 3 old joke old tune piece
of the street televison radio and program tape recorder 3
into the argument

tape recorder 1   i waited up for you until two o'clock
last night

tape recorder 3   what we want to know is who put the
sand in the spinach

the use of irrelevant response will be found effective in
breaking obsessional association tracks   all association
tracks are obsessional   get it out of your head and into
the machines   stop arguing stop complaining stop talking let the machines argue   complain and talk   a tape
recorder is an externalized section of the human nervous

system   you can find out more about the nervous system
and gain more control over your reactions by using the
tape recorder than you could find out sitting twenty years
in the lotus posture or wasting your time on the analytic
couch

listen to your present time tapes and you will begin to
see who you are and what you are doing here   mix yesterday in with today and hear tomorrow your future rising
out of old recordings   you are a programmed tape recorder
set to record and play back

who programs you

who decides what tapes play back in present time

who plays back your old humiliations and defeats holding you in prerecorded preset time

you don't have to listen to that sound   you can program your own playback   you can decide what tapes
you want played back in present time   study your associational patterns and find out what cases in what prerecordings for playback program those old tapes out
it's all done with tape recorders there are many things
you can do with programmed tape recorders stage per-
formances programmed at arbitrary intervals so each performance is unpredictable and unique allowing any
degree of audience participation readings concerts programmed tape recorders can create a happening anywhere
programmed tape recorders are of course essential to any
party and no modern host would bore his guests with a
straight present time party in a modern house every
room is bugged recorders record and play back from hidden mikes and loudspeakers phantom voices mutter
through corridors and rooms word visible as a haze tape
recorders in the gardens answer each other like barking
dogs sound track brings the studio on set you can change
the look of a city by putting your own sound track into
the streets here are some experiments filming a sound
track operations on set find a neighborhood with slate
roofs and red brick chimneys cool grey sound track fog

horns distant train whistles frogs croaking music across the golf course cool blue recordings in a cobblestone market with blue shutters all the sad old showmen stand there in blue twilight a rustle of darkness and wires when several thousand people working with tape recorders and filming subsequent action select their best sound tracks and film footage and splice together you will see something interesting now consider the harm that can be done and has been done when recording and playback is expertly carried out in such a way that the people effected do not know what is happening thought feeling and apparent sensory impressions can be precisely manipulated and controlled riots and demonstrations to order for example they use old anti-semitic recordings against the chinese in indonesia run shop and get rich and always give the business to another tiddly wink pretty familiar suppose you want to bring down the area go in and record all the ugliest stupidest dialogue the most discordant sound track you can find and keep playing it back which will occasion more ugly stupid dialogue recorded and played back on and on always selecting the ugliest material possibilities are unlimited you want to start a riot put your machines in the street with riot recordings move fast enough you can stay just ahead of the riot surf boarding we call it no margin for error recollect poor old burns caught out in a persian market riot recordings hid under his jellaba and they skinned him alive raw peeled thing writhing there in the noon sun and we got the picture

do you get the picture

the techniques and experiments described here have been used and are being used by agencies official and non-official without your awareness and very much to your disadvantage any number can play wittgenstein said no proposition can contain itself as an argument the only thing not prerecorded on a prerecorded set is the prerecording itself that is any recording in which a random

factor operates any street recording you can prerecord
your future   you can hear and see what you want to hear
and see   the experiments described here were explained
and demonstrated to me by ian sommerville of london in
this article i am writing as his ghost

look around you   look at a control machine programmed
to select the ugliest stupidest most vulgar and degraded
sounds for recording and playback which provokes uglier
stupider more vulgar and degraded sounds to be recorded
and play back inexorable degradation   look forward to
dead end   look forward to ugly vulgar playback tomorrow and tomorrow and tomorrow what are newspapers
doing but selecting the ugliest sounds for playback by and
large if its ugly its news and if that isn't enough i quote
from the editorial page of the new york daily news   we
can take care of china and if russia intervenes we can
take care of that nation too the only good communist is a
dead communist lets take care of slave driver castro next
what are we waiting for let's bomb china now and let's
stay armed to the teeth for centuries this ugly vulgar bray
put out for mass playback you want to spread hysteria
record and play back the most stupid and hysterical reactions

marijuana   marijuana   why that's deadlier than cocaine
it will turn a man into a homicidal maniac he said
steadily his eyes cold as he thought of the vampires who
suck riches from the vile traffic in pot quite literally
swollen with human blood   he reflected grimly and his
jaw set pushers should be pushed into the electric chair
strip the bastards naked
all right let's see your arms
or in the mortal words of harry j anslinger   the laws
must reflect society's disapproval of the addict
an uglier reflection than society's disapproval would be
hard to find the mean cold eyes of decent american
women tight lips and no thank you from the shop keeper
snarling cops pale nigger killing eyes reflecting society's

disapproval fucking queers i say shoot them if on the
other hand you select calm sensible reactions for recordings and playback you will spread calmness and good
sense

is this being done

obviously it is not only way to break the inexorable
down spiral of ugly uglier ugliest recording and playback
is with counterrecording and playback the first step is to
isolate and cut association lines of the control machine
carry a tape recorder with you and record all the ugliest
stupidest things cut your ugly tapes in together speed up
slow down play backwards inch the tape you will hear
one ugly voice and see one ugly spirit is made of ugly
old prerecordings the more you run the tapes through
and cut them up the less power they will have cut the
prerecordings into air into thin air*

As I have indicated in the *invisible generation* a technique for directing thought and producing events on a
mass scale is available to anyone with a portable recorder
or a car to transport recorders. The basis for this technique
is waking suggestion first used by Doctor John Dent of
London who also introduced the apomorphine treatment
for alcoholism and drug addiction.

Waking suggestion as practiced by Doctor Dent: The
patient is instructed to read aloud from a book while concentrating his attention on what he is reading as if reading
to an imaginary person sitting in front of him. The doctor
stands behind the patient and repeats at the same voice
level as the patient is using certain suggestions previously
agreed upon between doctor and patient. . .("You will be
able to sleep. You will not relapse into the use of alcohol
etc."). . . The patient, since he is reading aloud and his
attention is concentrated on what he is reading, does not
hear the suggestions consciously and for this reason they

* William S. Burroughs, *The Ticket That Exploded* (New York:
Grove Press, 1967).

take direct effect on his unconscious or reactive mind. *This is not subliminal suggestion.* Subliminal means below the conscious level of sight or hearing. Even if the subject were concentrating all his attention on the source of subliminal sound or images he would not be able to see or hear anything consciously. Waking suggestion consists of sounds or images that are not consciously registered *since the subject's attention is elsewhere.* If his attention were directed toward the source he would be able to see or hear it immediately.

Waking suggestion not subliminal suggestion is the technique used in playback of pre-recorded tapes in the street, cocktail parties, bars, stations, airports, parks, subways, political rallies, theatre intermissions, etc. People do not consciously hear the taped suggestions because their attention is directed toward something else: crossing street, catching train, listening for plane call, listening to speaker, looking at TV, talking to companions. The volume level of the tape is adjusted to street sounds, speech level, etc. and a well-constructed suggestion tape will have pre-recorded street sounds or whatever cut in according to location.

Any suggestion tape is made much more effective if it contains contradictory commands. Such commands as "To stay here to stay there, to stop to go, to do it now to do it later, to turn right to turn left, to stay in to stay out, to slow down to speed up, permitted prohibited, to be right to be wrong, to stay present in the now, to stay absent in the future the past, to hurry to wait etc."

These commands are constantly being imposed by the environment. If for example your suggestion tape contains the phrases: "Look at that light in front of you. STOP ... Stay here... Be there..." and is played back to people waiting at a STOP light they are *forced to obey the suggestion you are making.* Furthermore any contradictory commands at the unconscious level produce a moment of disorientation during which your suggestions take effect.

Suggestion tapes that contain contradictory commands have much more force than those that do not. Insult tape with contradictory commands cut in are particularly effective.

Results are obtained by constant playback of carefully prepared tapes. All tape-recorder tricks are useful: echo chamber for stations and air terminals, overlay, speed-up, slow-down, oscillation etc. Getting results is a matter of persistence and experimentation. For wide coverage use a car cutting in your suggestion tapes with popular tunes and street sounds. Some situations can only be covered on foot. When playing back insult tapes the operator is well advised to move quickly and stay out of his wake.

Q : For you, drugs are the most important medical problems of our time, and you constantly emphasize their horrors. "Everything that can be obtained chemically can be obtained otherwise as well."

A : As regards nonchemical methods of increasing awareness I have already described some tape-recorder experiments. Additional answers to this question? I submit an article by Mr Brion Gysin on the Dreammachine, an article on the use of hieroglyphs, entitled *Scribe Street*, and one on the use of projections, entitled *How to be Humphrey Bogart*, the latter two by myself.

The Dreammachine, developed by Brion Gysin and Ian Sommerville, is a pierced cylinder, which whirls around a light source to produce stroboscopic "flicker" over the closed eyelids of the viewer. "Flicker" at precise rates per second produces radical change in the "alpha" or scanning rhythms of the brain as shown by electroencephalographic research. Subjects report dazzling lights of unearthly brilliance and color, developing in magnitude and complexity of pattern as long as the stimulation lasts. When the flicker is in phase with the subject's alpha rhythms he sees extending areas of colored pattern which develop throughout the entire visual field, 360 degrees of hallucinatory vision in which constellations of images appear. Elaborate geometric constructions of incredible intricacy build up from multidimensional mosaic into living fireballs like the *mandalas* of Eastern mysticism or resolve momentarily into apparently individual images and powerfully dramatic scenes like brightly colored dreams.

Our ancestors saw the creatures of the constellations in the apparently unorganized distribution of the stars. It has been shown experimentally through the viewing of random white dots on a screen that man tends to find pattern and picture where objectively there is none: his mental process shapes what it sees. The alpha rhythms, at about 13 per second, are our scanning speeds which may vary from one individual to another or according to age and, perhaps, culture. They are strongest when the brain is unoccupied, searching for pattern which may be aural, traveling at the speed of sound or visual, traveling at the speed of light. Rhythmic sound, films and TV impose external rhythms on the mind, altering the brain waves which have been otherwise as individual as our fingerprints, at least. It is entirely possible that the EEG records of a generation of TV watchers will be similar, even identical.

An oral society; traveling at the low speed of sound, might function in the dark. In the beginning was the word and the word was made flesh in darkness, but, with the invention of writing in any form, light was necessary to see the image which became another form of proliferation whose limits are the speed of light. The one and only thing which cannot be taken from the picture is light—everything else can be utterly transmuted or can go.

Change is a function of number and, today in the electronic age, our only interesting constant is 186,000 miles per second; the speed of light, which the speed of electricity does not reach let alone surpass. The word, then, is at its slowest when spoken, 1114 feet per second; the speed of sound at its fastest when seen or projected as an image at the speed of light. But our alpha or scanning rhythms of the brain are weakest during purposeful thinking, eyes open, studying pattern and slowest of all during reading which is the decipherment of a series of meaningful patterns.

"Flicker" is a threshold experience of induced experience produced by altering the speed of light to accommodate the maximum range of our alpha rhythms. "Flicker" creates a dazzling multiplicity of images in constantly altering relationships which makes the "collages" and "assemblages" of so-called "modern" art appear utterly ineffectual and slow. Art history is no longer being created. Art history as the enumeration of individual images ended with the direct introduction of light as the principal agent in the creation of images which have become infinitely multiple, complex and all-pervading. The comet is Light.

ELECTRONIC REVOLUTION 1970–71

In "The Invisible Generation" first published in IT and in the *Los Angeles Free Press* in 1966, I consider the potential of thousands of people with recorders, portable and stationary, messages passed along like signal drums, a parody of the President's speech up and down the balconies, in and out open windows, through walls, over courtyards, taken up by barking dogs, muttering bums, music, traffic down windy streets, across parks and soccer fields. Illusion is a revolutionary weapon. To point out some specific uses of prerecorded cut/up tapes played back in the streets as a revolutionary weapon:

To spread rumors
Put ten operators with carefully prepared recordings out at the rush hour and see how quick the words gets around. People don't know where they heard it but they heard it.

To discredit opponents

Take a recorded Wallace speech, cut in stammering coughs sneezes hiccoughs snarls pain screams fear whimperings apoplectic sputterings slobbering drooling idiot noises sex and animal sound effects and play it back in the streets subways stations parks political rallies.

As a front line weapon to produce and escalate riots

There is nothing mystical about this operation. Riot sound effects can produce an actual riot in a riot situation. *Recorded police whistles will draw cops. Recorded gunshots, and their guns are out.*

"MY GOD, THEY'RE KILLING US."

A guardsman said later: "I heard the shots and saw my buddy go down, his face covered in blood (turned out he'd been hit by a stone from a sling shot) and I thought, well this is it." BLOODY WEDNESDAY. A DAZED AMERICA COUNTED 23 DEAD AND 32 WOUNDED, 6 CRITICALLY.

Here is a run of the mill, pre-riot situation. Protestors have been urged to demonstrate peacefully, police and guardsmen to exercise restraint. Ten tape recorders strapped under their coats, play back and record controlled from lapel buttons. They have prerecorded riot sound effects from Chicago, Paris, Mexico City, Kent, Ohio. If they adjust sound level of recordings to surrounding sound levels, they will not be detected. Police scuffle with the demonstrators. The operators converge. Turn on Chicago record, play back, move on to the next scuffles, record, play back, keep moving. Things are hotting up, a cop is down groaning. Shrill chorus of recorded pig squeals and parody groans.

Could you cool a riot recording the calmest cop and the most reasonable demonstrators? Maybe! However, it's a lot easier to start trouble than stop it. Just pointing out that cut/ups on the tape recorder can be used as a weapon. You'll observe that the operators are making a cutup as they go. They are cutting in Chicago, Paris, Mexico City,

Kent, Ohio with the present sound effects at random, and that is a cutup.

As a long range weapon to scramble and nullify associational lines put down by mass media

The control of the mass media depends on laying down lines of association. When the lines are cut the associational connections are broken.

President Johnson burst into a swank apartment, held three maids at gunpoint, 26 miles north of Saigon yesterday.

You can cut the mutter line of the mass media and put the altered mutter line out in the streets with a tape recorder. Consider the mutter line of the daily press. It goes up with the morning papers, millions of people reading the same words, belching chewing swearing chuckling reacting to the same words. In different ways, of course. A motion praising Mr. Callaghan's action in banning the South African Cricket Tour has spoiled the colonel's breakfast. All reacting one way or another to the paper world of unseen events which becomes an integral part of your reality. You will notice that this process is continually subject to random juxtaposition. Just what sign did you see in the Green Park station as you glanced up from the *People?* Just who called as you were reading your letter in the *Times?* What were you reading when your wife broke a dish in the kitchen? An unreal paper world and yet completely real because it is actually happening. Mutter line of the *Evening News*, TV. Fix yourself on millions of people all watching Jesse James or the Virginian at the same time. International mutter line of the weekly news magazine always dated a week ahead. Have you noticed it's the kiss of death to be on the front cover of *Time*. Madam Nhu was there when her husband was killed and her government fell. Verwoerd was on the front cover of *Time* when a demon tapeworm gave the order for his death through a messenger of the same. Read the Bible, kept to himself, no bad habits, you know the type. Old reliable, read all about it.

So stir in news stories, TV plays, stock market quotations, adverts and put the altered mutter line out in the streets.

The underground press serves as the only effective counter to a growing power and more sophisticated techniques used by establishment mass media to falsify, misrepresent, misquote, rule out of consideration as a *priori* ridiculous or simply ignore and blot out of existence: data, books, discoveries that they consider prejudicial to establishment interest.

I suggest that the underground press could perform this function much more effectively by the use of cut/up techniques. For example, prepare cut/ups of the ugliest reactionary statements you can find and surround them with the ugliest pictures. Now give it the drool, slobber, animal-noise treatment and put it out on the mutter line with recorders. Run a scramble page in every issue of a transcribed tape recorded cut/up of news, radio, and TV. Put the recordings out on the mutter line before the paper hits the stand. It gives you a funny feeling to see a headline that's been going round and round in your head. The underground press could add a mutter line to their adverts and provide a unique advertising service. Cut the product in with pop tunes, cut the product in with advertising slogans and jingles of other products and syphon off the sales. Anybody who doubts that these techniques work has only to put them to the test. The techniques here described are in use by the CIA and agents of other countries. Ten years ago they were making systematic street recordings in every district of Paris. I recall the Voice of America man in Tangier and a room full of tape recorders and you could hear some strange sounds through the wall. Kept to himself, hello in the hall. Nobody was ever allowed in that room, not even a fatima. Of course, there are many technical elaborations like long-range directional mikes. When cutting the prayer call in with hog grunts it doesn't pay to be walking around the market place with a portable tape recorder.

An article in *New Scientist* June 4, 1970, page 470, entitled "Electronic Arts of Noncommunication" by Richard C. French gives the clue for more precise technical instructions.

In 1968, with the help of Ian Sommerville and Anthony Balch, I took a short passage of my recorded voice and cut it into intervals of one twenty-fourth of a second on movie tape—(movie tape is larger and easier to splice)—and rearranged the order of the 24th second intervals of recorded speech. The original words are quite unintelligible but new words emerge. The voice is still there and you can immediately recognize the speaker. Also the tone of voice remains. If the tone is friendly, hostile, sexual, poetic, sarcastic, lifeless, despairing, this will be apparent in the altered sequence.

I did not realize at the time that I was using a technique that has been in existence since 1881 . . . I quote from Mr. French's article . . . "Designs for speech scramblers go back to 1881 and the desire to make telephone and radio communications unintelligible to third parties has been with us ever since" . . . The message is scrambled in transmission and then unscrambled at the other end. There are many of these speech scrambling devices that work on different principles . . . "Another device which saw service during the war was the time division scrambler. The signal is chopped up into elements .005cm long. These elements are taken in groups or frames and rearranged in a new sequence. Imagine that the speech recorded is recorded on magnetic tape which is cut into pieces .02 long and the pieces rearranged into a new sequence. This can actually be done and gives a good idea what speech sounds like when scrambled in this way."

This I had done in 1968. And this is an extension of the cut/up method. The simplest cut/up cuts a page down the middle into four sections. Section 1 is then placed with section 4 and section 3 with section 2 in a new sequence. Carried further we can break the page down into smaller and smaller units in altered sequences.

The original purpose of scrambling devices was to make the message unintelligible without the unscrambling code.

Another use for speech scramblers could be to impose thought control on a mass scale. Consider the human body and nervous system as unscrambling devices. A common virus like the cold sore could sensitize the subject to unscramble messages. Drugs like LSD and Dim-N could also act as unscrambling devices. Moreover, the mass media could sensitize millions of people to receive scrambled versions of the same set of data. Remember that when the human nervous system unscrambles a scrambled message this will seem to the subject like his very own ideas which just occurred to him, which indeed it did.

Take a card, any card. In most cases he will not suspect its extraneous origin. That is the run of the mill newspaper reader who receives the scrambled message uncritically and assumes that it reflects his own opinions independently arrived at. On the other hand, the subject may recognize or suspect the extraneous origin of voices that are literally hatching out in his head. Then we have the classic syndrome of paranoid psychosis. Subject hears voices. Anyone can be made to hear voices with scrambling techniques. It is not difficult to expose him to the actual scrambled message, any part of which can be made intelligible. This can be done with street recorders, recorders in cars, doctored radio and TV sets. In his own flat if possible, if not in some bar or restaurant he frequents. If he doesn't talk to himself, he soon will do. You bug his flat. Now he is really round the bend hearing his own voice out of radio and TV broadcasts and the conversation of passing strangers. See how easy it is? Remember the scrambled message is partially unintelligible and in any case he gets the tone. Hostile white voices unscrambled by a Negro will also activate by association every occasion on which he has been threatened or humiliated by whites. To carry it further you can use recordings of voices known to him. You can turn him against his friends by hostile scrambled messages in a friend's voice. This will activate all his disagreements with that friend. You can condition him to like his enemies by friendly scrambled messages in enemy voices.

On the other hand the voices can be friendly and reassuring. He is now working for the CIA, the GPU, or whatever, and these are his orders. They now have an agent who has no information to give away and who doesn't have to be paid. And he is now completely under control. If he doesn't obey orders they can give him the hostile voice treatment. No, "They" are not God or super technicians from outer space. Just technicians operating with well-known equipment and using techniques that can be duplicated by anybody else who can buy and operate this equipment.

To see how scrambling technique could work on a mass media scale, imagine that a news magazine like Time got out a whole issue a week before publication and filled it with news based on predictions following a certain line, without attempting the impossible, giving our boys a boost in every story and the Commies as many defeats and casualties as possible, a whole issue of Time formed from slanted prediction of future news. Now imagine this scrambled out through the mass media.

With minimal equipment you can do the same thing on a smaller scale. You need a scrambling device, TV, radio, two video cameras, a ham radio station and a simple photo studio with a few props and actors. For a start you scramble the news all together and spit it out every which way on ham radio and street recorders. You construct fake news broadcasts on video camera. For the pictures you can use mostly old footage. Mexico City will do for a riot in Saigon and vice versa. For a riot in Santiago, Chile you can use the Londonderry pictures. Nobody knows the difference. Fires, earthquakes, plane crashes can be moved around. For example, here is a plane crash, 112 dead north of Barcelona and here is a plane crash in Toronto 108 dead. So move the picture of the Barcelona plane crash over to Toronto and Toronto to Barcelona. And you scramble your fabricated news in with actual news broadcasts.

You have an advantage which your opposing player

does not have. He must conceal his manipulations. You are under no such necessity. In fact you can advertise the fact that you are writing news in advance and trying to make it happen by techniques which anybody can use. And that makes you NEWS. And a TV personality as well, if you play it right. You want the widest possible circulation for your cut/up video tapes. Cut/up techniques could swamp the mass media with total illusion.

Fictional dailies retroactively cancelled the San Francisco earthquake and the Halifax explosion as journalistic hoaxes, and doubt released from the skin law extendable and ravenous, consumed all the facts of history.

Mr. French concludes his article . . . "The use of modern microelectric integrated circuits could lower the cost of speech scramblers enough to see them in use by private citizens. Codes and ciphers have always had a strong appeal to most people and I think scramblers will as well . . ."

It is generally assumed that speech must be consciously understood to cause an effect. Early experiments with subliminal images have shown that this is not true. A number of research projects could be based on speech scramblers. We have all seen the experiment where someone speaking hears his own recorded voice back a few seconds later. Soon he cannot go on talking. Would scrambled speech have the same effect? To what extent are scrambled messages actually unscrambled by experimental subjects? To what extent does a language act as an unscrambling device, western languages tending to unscramble in either-or conflict terms? To what extent does the tone of voice used by a speaker impose a certain unscrambling sequence on the listener?

Many of the cut/up tapes would be entertaining and in fact entertainment is the most promising field for cut/up techniques. Imagine a pop festival like Phun City scheduled for July 24th, 25th, 26th, 1970 at Ecclesden Common, Patching, near Worthing, Sussex. Festival area comprised of car park and camping area, a rock auditorium, a village with booths and cinema, a large wooded area. A number of tape recorders are planted in the woods and the village. As many as possible so as to lay down a grid of sound over the whole festival. Recorders have tapes of prerecorded material, music, news broadcasts, recordings from other festivals, etc. At all times some of the recorders are playing back and some are recording. The recorders recording at any time are of course recording the crowd and the other tape recorders that are playing back at varying distances. This cuts in the crowd who will be hearing their own voices back. Play back, wind back and record could be electronically controlled with varying intervals. Or they could be hand operated, the operator deciding what intervals of play back, record, and wind back to use. Effect is greatly increased by a large number of festival goers with portable recorders playing back and recording as they walk around the festival. We can carry it further with projection screens and video cameras. Some of the material projected is pre-prepared, sex films, films of other festivals, and this material is cut in with live TV broadcasts and shots of the crowd. Of course, the rock festival will be cut in on the screens, thousands of fans with portable recorders recording and playing back, the singer could direct play back and record. Set up an area for travelling performers, jugglers, animal acts, snake charmers, singers, musicians, and cut these acts in. Film and tape from the festival, edited for the best material, could then be used at other festivals.

Quite a lot of equipment and engineering to set it up. The festival could certainly be enhanced if as many festival goers as possible bring portable tape recorders to record and play back at the festival.

Any message, music, conversation you want to pass around, bring it pre-recorded on tape so everybody takes pieces of your tape home.

Research project: to find out to what extent scrambled messages are unscrambled, that is scanned out by experimental subjects. The simplest experiment consists in playing back a scrambled message to subject. Message could contain simple commands. Does the scrambled message have any command value comparable to post-hypnotic suggestion? Is the actual content of the message received? What drugs, if any, increase ability to unscramble messages? Do subjects vary widely in this ability? Are scrambled messages in the subject's own voice more effective than messages in other voices? Are messages scrambled in certain voices more easily unscrambled by specific subjects? Is the message more potent with both word and image scrambled on video tape? Now to use, for example, a video-tape message with a unified emotional content. Let us say the message is fear. For this we take all the past fear shots of the subject we can collect or evoke. We cut these in with fear words and pictures, with threats, etc. This is all acted out and would be upsetting enough in any case. Now let's try it scrambled and see if we get an even stronger effect. The subject's blood pressure, rate of heart beat, and brain waves are recorded as we play back the scrambled tape. His face is photographed and visible to him on video camera at all times. The actual scrambling of the tape can be done in two ways. It can be a completely random operation like pulling pieces out of a hat and if this is done several consecutive units may occur together, yielding an identifiable picture or intelligible word. Both methods of course can be used at varying intervals. Blood pressure, heart beat, and brain-wave recordings will show the operator what material is producing the strongest reaction, and he will of course zero in. And remember that the subject can see his face at all times and his face is being photographed. As the Peeping Tom said, the most frightening thing is fear in your own face. If the subject becomes too disturbed we have peace and safety tapes ready.

Now here is a sex tape: this consists of a sex scene acted out by the ideal sexual object of the subject and his ideal self image. Shown straight it might be exciting enough, now scramble it. It takes a few seconds for scrambled tapes to hatch out, and then? Can scrambled sex tapes zeroing in on the subject's reactions and brain waves result in spontaneous orgasm? Can this be extended to other functions of the body? A mike secreted in the water closet and all his shits and farts recorded and scrambled in with stern nanny voices commanding him to shit, and the young liberal shits in his pants on the platform right under Old Glory. Could laugh tapes, sneeze tapes, hiccough tapes, cough tapes, give rise to laughing, sneezing, hiccoughing, and coughing?

To what extent can physical illness be induced by scrambled illness tapes? Take, for example, a sound and color picture of a subject with a cold. Later, when subject is fully recovered, we take color and sound film of recovered subject. We now scramble the cold pictures and sound track in with present sound and image track. We also project the cold pictures on present pictures. Now we try using some of Mr. Hubbard's reactive mind phrases which are supposed in themselves to produce illness. To be me, to be you, to stay here, to stay there, to be a body, to be bodies, to stay present, to stay past. Now we scramble all this in together and show it to the subject. Could seeing and hearing this sound and image track, scrambled down to very small units, bring about an attack of cold virus? If such a cold tape does actually produce an attack of cold virus we cannot say that we have created a virus, perhaps we have merely activated a latent virus. Many viruses, as you know, are latent in the body and may be activated. We can try the same with coldsore, with hepatitis, always remembering that we may be activating a latent virus and in no sense creating a laboratory virus. However, we may be in a position to do this. Is a virus perhaps simply very small units of sound and image? Remember the only image a virus has is the image and sound track it can impose on you. The yellow eyes of jaundice, the pustules of smallpox, etc. imposed on you against your will. The same is certainly true of scrambled word and image, its existence is the word and image it can make you unscramble. Take a card, any card. This does not mean that it is actually a virus. Perhaps to construct a laboratory virus we would need both camera and sound crew and a biochemist as well. I quote from the *International Paris Tribune* an article on the synthetic gene: "Dr. Har Johrd Khorana has made a gene-synthetic."

"It is the beginning of the end," this was the immediate reaction to this news from the science attaché at one of Washington's major embassies. "If you can make genes you can eventually make new viruses for which there are no cures. Any little country with good biochemists could make such biological weapons. It would take only a small laboratory. If it can be done, somebody will do it." For example, a death virus could be created that carries the coded message of death. A death tape, in fact. No doubt the technical details are complex and perhaps a team of sound and camera men working with biochemists would give us the answer.

And now the question as to whether scrambling techniques could be used to spread helpful and pleasant messages. Perhaps. On the other hand, the scrambled words and tape act like a virus in that they force something on the subject against his will. More to the point would be to discover how the old scanning patterns could be altered so that the subject liberates his own spontaneous scanning pattern.

New Scientist, 2 July, 1970 . . . Current memory theory posits a seven second temporary "buffer store" preceding the main one: a blow on the head wipes out memory of this much prior time because it erases the contents of the buffer. Daedalus observes that the sense of the present also covers just this range and so suggests that our sensory input is in effect recorded on an endless time loop, providing some seven seconds of delay for scanning before erasure. In this time the brain edits, makes sense of, and selects for storage key features. The weird *déjà* vu sensation that "now" has happened before is clearly due to brief erasure failure, so that we encounter already stored memory data coming round again. Time dragging or racing must reflect tape speed. A simple experiment will demonstrate this erasure process in operation. Making street recordings and playing them back, you will hear things you do not remember, sometimes said in a loud clear voice, must have been quite close to you, nor do you necessarily remember them when you hear the recording back. The sound has been erased according to a scanning pattern which is automatic. This means that what you notice and store as memory as you walk down a street is scanned out of a much larger selection of data which is then erased from the memory. For the walker the signs he passed, people he has passed, are erased from his mind and cease to exist for him. Now to make this scanning process conscious and controllable, try this:

Walk down a city block with a camera and take what you notice, moving the camera around as closely as possible to follow the direction of your eyes. The point is to make the camera your eyes and take what your eyes are scanning out of the larger picture. At the same time take the street at wide angle from a series of still positions. The street of the operator is, of course, the street as seen by the operator. It is different from the street seen at wide angle. Much of it is in fact missing. Now you can make arbitrary scanning patterns—that is cover first one side of the street and then the other in accordance with a preconceived plan. So you are breaking down the automatic scanning patterns. You could also make color scanning patterns, that is, scan out green, blue, red, etc. in so far as you can with your camera. That is, you are using an arbitrary preconceived scanning pattern, in order to break down automatic scanning patterns. A number of operators do this and then scramble in their takes together and with wide angle tapes. This could train the subject to see at a wider angle and also to ignore and erase at will.

Now, all this is readily subject to experimental verification on control subjects. Nor need the equipment be all that complicated. I have shown how it could work with feedback from brain waves and visceral response and video tape photos of subject taken while he is seeing and hearing the tape, simply to show optimum effectiveness. You can start with two tape recorders. The simplest scrambling device is scissors and splicing equipment. You can start scrambling words, make any kind of tapes and scramble them and observe the effects on friends and on yourself. Next step is sound film and then video camera. Of course results from individual experiments could lead to mass experiments, mass fear tapes, riot tapes, etc. The possibilities here for research and experiment are virtually unlimited and I have simply made a few very simple suggestions.

"A virus is characterised and limited by obligate cellular parasitism. All viruses must parasitise living cells for their replication. For all viruses the infection cycle comprises entry into the host, intracellular replication, and escape from the body of the host to initiate a new cycle in a fresh host." I am quoting here from *Mechanisms of Virus Infection* edited by Dr. Wilson Simth. In its wild state the virus has not proved to be a very adaptable organism. Some viruses have burned themselves out since they were 100 per cent fatal and there were no reservoirs. Each strain of virus is rigidly programmed for a certain attack on certain tissues. If the attack fails, the virus does not gain a new host. There are, of course, virus mutations, and the influenza virus has proved quite versatile in this way. Generally it's the simple repetition of the same method of entry, and if that method is blocked by any body or other agency such as interferon, the attack fails. By and large, our virus is a stupid organism. Now we can think for the virus, devise a number of alternate methods of entry. For example, the host is simultaneously attacked by an ally virus who tells him that everything is alright and by a pain and fear virus. So the virus is now using an old method of entry, namely, the tough cop and the con cop.

We have considered the possibility that a virus can be activated or even created by very small units of sound and image. So conceived, the virus can be made to order in the laboratory. Ah, but for the takes to be effective, you must have also the actual virus and what is this so actual virus? New viruses turn up from time to time but from where do they turn up? Well, let's see how we could make a virus turn up. We plot now our virus's symptoms and make a scramble tape. The most susceptible subjects, that is those who reproduce some of the desired symptoms, will then be scrambled into more tapes till we scramble our virus into existence. This birth of a virus occurs when our virus is able to reproduce itself in a host and pass itself on to another host. Perhaps, too, with the virus under laboratory control it can be tamed for useful purposes. Imagine, for example, a sex virus. It so inflames the sex centers in the back brain that the host is driven mad from sexuality, all other considerations are blacked out. Parks full of naked, frenzied people, shitting, pissing, ejaculating, and screaming. So the virus could be malignant, blacking out all regulation and end in exhaustion, convulsions, and death.

Now let us attempt the same thing with tape. We organize a sex-tape festival. 100,000 people bring their scrambled sex tapes, and video tapes as well, to scramble in together. Projected on vast screens, muttering out over the crowd, sometimes it slows down so you see a few seconds, then scrambled again, then slow down, scramble. Soon it will scramble them all naked. The cops and the National Guard are stripping down. LET'S GET OURSELVES SOME CIVVIES. Now a thing like that could be messy, but those who survive it recover from the madness. Or, say, a small select group of really like-minded people get together with their sex tapes, you see the process is now being brought under control. And the fact that anybody can do it is in itself a limiting factor.

Here is Mr. Hart, who wants to infect everyone with his own image and turn them all into himself, so he scrambles himself and dumps himself out in search of worthy vessels. If nobody else knows about scrambling techniques he might scramble himself quite a stable of replicas. But anybody can do it. So go on, scramble your sex words out, and find suitable mates.

If you want to, scramble yourself out there, every stale joke, fart, chew, sneeze, and stomach rumble. If your

189 · *Academy 23*

trick no work you better run. Everybody doing it, they all scramble in together and the populations of the earth just settle down a nice even brown color. Scrambles is the democratic way, the way of full cellular representation. Scrambles is the American way.

I have suggested that virus can be created to order in the laboratory from very small units of sound and image. Such a preparation is not in itself biologically active but it could activate or even create virus in susceptible subjects. A carefully prepared jaundice tape could activate or create the jaundice virus in liver cells, especially in cases where the liver is already damaged. The operator is in effect directing a virus revolution of the cells. Since DOR seems to attack those exposed to it at the weakest point, release of this force could coincide with virus attack. Reactive mind phrases could serve the same purpose of rendering subjects more susceptible to virus attack.

It will be seen that scrambled speech already has many of the characteristics of virus. When the speech takes and unscrambles, this occurs compulsively and against the will of the subject. A virus must remind you of its presence. Whether it is the nag of a cold sore or the torturing spasms of rabies the virus reminds you of its unwanted presence. "HERE ME IS."

So does scrambled word and image. The units are unscrambling compulsively, presenting certain words and images to the subject and this repetitive presentation is irritating certain bodily and neutral areas. The cells so irritated can produce over a period of time the biologic virus units. We now have a new virus that can be communicated and indeed the subject may be desperate to communicate this thing that is bursting inside him. He is heavy with the load. Could this load be good and beautiful? Is it possible to create a virus which will communicate calm and sweet reasonableness? A virus must parasitise a host in order to survive. It uses the cellular material of the host to make copies of itself. In most cases this is damaging to the host. The virus gains entrance by fraud and maintains itself by force. An unwanted guest who makes you sick to look at is never good or beautiful. It is moreover a guest who always repeats itself word for word take for take.

Remember the life cycle of a virus . . . penetration of a cell or activation within the cell, replication within the cell, escape from cell to invade other cells, escape from host to infect a new host. This infection can take place in many ways and those who find themselves heavy with the load of a new virus generally use a shotgun technique to cover a wide range of infection routes . . . cough, sneeze, spit and fart at every opportunity. Save shit, piss, snot, scabs, sweat stained clothes and all bodily secretions for dehydration. The composite dust can be unobtrusively billowed out a roach bellows in subways, dropped from windows in bags, or sprayed out a crop duster . . . Carry with you at all times an assortment of vectors . . . lice, fleas, bed bugs, and little aviaries of mosquitoes and biting flies filled with your blood . . . I see no beauty in that.

There is only one case of a favorable virus influence benefiting an obscure species of Australian mice. On the other hand, if a virus produces no damaging symptoms we have no way of ascertaining its existence and this happens with latent virus infections. It has been suggested that yellow races resulted from a jaundice-like virus which produced a permanent mutation not necessarily damaging, which was passed along genetically. The same may be true of the word. The word itself may be a virus that has achieved a permanent status with the host. However, no known virus in existence at the present time acts in this manner, so the question of a beneficent virus remains open. It seems advisable to concentrate on a general defense against all virus.

Ron Hubbard, founder of scientology, says that certain words and word combinations can produce serious illnesses and mental disturbances. I can claim some skill in the scrivener's trade, but I cannot guarantee to write a passage that will make someone physically ill. If Mr. Hubbard's claim is justified, this is certainly a matter for further research, and we can easily find out experimentally whether his claim is justified or not. Mr. Hubbard bases the power he attributes to words on his theory of engrams. An engram is defined as word, sound, image recorded by the subject in a period of pain and unconsciousness. Some of this material may be reassuring: "I think he's going to be alright." Reassuring material is an ally engram. Ally engrams, according to Mr. Hubbard, are just as bad as hostile pain engrams. Any part of this recording played back to the subject later will reactivate operation pain, he may actually develop a headache and feel depressed, anxious, or tense. Well, Mr. Hubbard's engram theory is very easily subject to experimental vertification. Take ten volunteer subjects, subject them to a pain stimulus accompanied by certain words and sounds and images. You can act out little skits.

"Quickly, nurse, before I lose my little nigger," bellows the southern surgeon, and now a beefy white hand falls on the fragile black shoulder. "Yes, he's going to be alright. He's going to pull through."

"If I had my way I'd let these animals die on the operating table."

"You do not have your way, you have your duty as a doctor, we must do everything in our power to save human lives."

And so forth.

It is the tough cop and the con cop. The ally engram is ineffective without the pain engram, just as the con cop's arm around your shoulder, his soft persuasive voice in your year, are indeed sweet nothings without the tough cop's blackjack. Now to what extent can words recorded during medical unconsciousness be recalled during hypnosis or scientological processing? To what extent does the playback of this material affect the subject unpleasantly? Is the effect enhanced by scrambling the material, pain and ally, at very short intervals? It would seem that a scrambled engram's picture could almost dump an operating scene right in the subject's lap. Mr. Hubbard has charted his version of what he calls the reactive mind. This is roughly similar to Freud's id, a sort of built-in self defeating mechanism. As set forth by Mr. Hubbard this consists of a number of quite ordinary phrases. He claims that reading these phrases, or hearing them spoken, can cause illness, and gives this as his reason for not publishing this material. Is he perhaps saying that these are magic words? Spells, in fact? If so they could be quite a weapon scrambled up with imaginative sound-and-image track. Here now is the magic that turns men into swine. To be an animal: a lone pig grunts, shits, squeals and slobbers down garbage. To be animals: a chorus of a thousand pigs. Cut that in with video tape police pictures and play it back to them and see if you get a reaction from this so reactive mind.

Now here is another. To be a body, well it's sure an attractive body, rope the marks in. And a nice body symphony to go with it, rhythmic heart beats, contented stomach rumbles. To be bodies: recordings and pictures of hideous, aged, diseased bodies farting, pissing, shitting, groaning, dying. To do everything: man in a filthy apartment surrounded by unpaid bills, unanswered letters, jumps up and starts washing dishes and writing letters. To do nothing: he slumps in a chair, jumps up, slumps in chair, jumps up. Finally, slumps in a chair, drooling in idiot helplessness, while he looks at the disorder piled around him. The reactive mind commands can also be used to advantage with illness tapes. While projecting past cold sore on to the subject's face, and playing back to him a past illness tape, you can say: to be me, to be you, to stay here, to stay there, to be a body, to be bodies, to stay in, to stay out, to stay present, to stay absent. To what extent are these reactive mind phrases when scrambled effective in causing disagreeable symptoms in control volunteer subjects? As to Mr. Hubbard's claims for the reactive mind, only research can give us the answers.

The RM then is an artifact designed to limit and stultify on a mass scale. In order to have this effect it must be widely implanted. This can readily be done with modern electronic equipment and the techniques described in this treatise. The RM consists of commands which seem harmless and in fact unavoidable . . . To be a body . . . but which can have the most horrific consequences.

Here are some sample RM screen effects . . .

As the theater darkens a bright light appears on the left side of the screen. The screen lights up

To be nobody . . . On screen shadow of ladder and soldier incinerated by the Hiroshima blast

To be everybody . . . Street crowds, riots, panics

To be me . . . A beautiful girl and a handsome young man point to selves

To be you . . . They point to audience . . .

Hideous hags and old men, lepers, drooling idiots point to themselves and to the audience as they intone . . .

To be me

To be you

Command no. 5 . . . To be myself

Command no. 6 . . . To be others

On screen a narcotics officer is addressing an audience of school boys. Spread out on a table in front of him are syringes, kief pipes, samples of heroin, hashiesh, LSD.

Officer: "Five trips on a drug can be a pleasant and exciting experience . . ."

On screen young trippers . . . "I'm really myself for the first time"

ETC happy trips . . . To be myself . . . no. 5 . . .

Officer: "THE SIXTH WILL PROBABLY BLOW YOUR HEAD OFF"

Shot shows a man blowing his head off with a shotgun in his mouth . . .

Officer: "Like a 15 year old boy I knew until recently,

you could well end up dying in your own spew . . . To be others no. 6 . . .

To be an animal . . . A lone Wolf Scout . . .

To be animals: He joins other wolf scouts playing, laughing, shouting

To be an animal . . . Bestial and ugly human behavior . . . brawls, disgusting eating and sex scenes

To be animals . . . Cows, sheep and pigs driven to the slaughter house

To be a body

To be bodies

A beautiful body . . . a copulating couple . . . Cut back and forth and run on seven second loop for several minutes . . . scramble at different speeds . . . Audience must be made to realize that to be a body is to be bodies . . . A body exists to be other bodies

To be a body . . . Death scenes and recordings . . . a scramble of last words

To be bodies . . . Vista of cemeteries . . .

To do it now . . . Couple embracing hotter and hotter

To do it now . . . A condemned cell . . . Condemned man is same actor as lover . . . He is led away by the guards screaming and struggling. Cut back and forth between sex scene and man led to execution. Couple in sex scene have orgasm as the condemned man is hanged, electrocuted, gassed, garrotted, shot in the head with a pistol

To do it later . . . The couple pull away . . . One wants to go out and eat and go to a show or something . . . They put on their hats . . .

To do it later . . . Warden arrives at condemned cell to tell the prisoner he has a stay of execution

To do it now . . . Grim faces in the Pentagon. Strategic is on its way . . . Well THIS IS IT . . . This sequence cut in with sex scenes and a condemned man led to execution, culminates in execution, orgasm, nuclear explosion . . . The condemned lover is a horribly burned survivor

To do it later . . . 1920 walk out sequence to "The

Sunny Side of the Street" . . . A disappointed general turns from the phone to say the President has opened top level hot wire talks with Russia and China . . . Condemned man gets another stay of execution

To be an animal . . . One lemming busily eating lichen . . .

To be animals . . . Hordes of lemmings swarming all over each other in mounting hysteria . . . A pile of drowned lemmings in front of somebody's nice little cottage on a Finnish lake where he is methodically going through sex positions with his girl friend. They wake up in a stink of dead lemmings

To be an animal . . . Little boy put on pot

To be animals . . . The helpless shitting infant is eaten alive by rats

To stay put . . . A man has just been hanged. The doctor steps forward with a stethoscope

To stay down . . . Body is carried out with the rope around neck . . . naked corpse on the autopsy table . . . corpse buried in quick lime

To stay up . . . Erect phallus

To stay down . . . White man burns off a Negro's genitals with blow torch . . . Theater darkens into the blow torch on left side of the screen

To stay present

To stay absent

To stay present . . . A boy masturbates in front of sex pictures . . . Cut to face of white man who is burning off black genitals with blow torch

To stay absent . . . Sex phantasies of the boy . . . The black slumps dead with genitals burned off and intestines popping out

To stay present . . . Boy watches strip tease, intent, fascinated . . . A man stands on trap about to be hanged

To stay present . . . Sex phantasies of the boy . . . "I pronounce this man dead"

To stay present . . . Boy whistles at girl in street . . . A man's body twists in the electric chair, his leg hairs crackling with blue fire

To stay absent . . . Boy sees himself in bed with girl
. . . Man slumps dead in chair smoke curling from under
the hood saliva dripping from his mouth . . .

The Theater lights up. In the sky a plane over Hiroshima
. . . Little Boy slides out

To stay present . . . The plane, the pilot, the American flag . . .

To stay absent . . . Theater darkens into atomic blast
on screen

Here we see ordinary men and women going about their
ordinary everyday jobs and diversions . . . subways, streets,
buses, trains, airports, stations, waiting rooms, homes, flats,
restaurants, offices, factories . . . working, eating, playing,
defecating, making love

A chorus of voices cuts in RM phrases

To stay up

To stay down

Elevators, airports, stairs, ladders

To stay in

To stay out

Street signs, door signs, people at head of lines admitted to restaurants and theaters

To be myself

To be others

Customs agents check passports, man identifies himself
at bank to cash check

To stay present

To stay absent

People watching films, reading, looking at TV . . .

A composite of this sound and image track is now run
on seven second loop without change for several minutes.

Now cut in the horror pictures

To stay up

To stay down

Elevators, airports, stairs, ladders, hangings, castrations

To stay in

To stay out

Door signs, operation scenes . . . doctor tosses bloody
tonsils, adenoids, appendix into receptacle

To stay present
To stay absent
People watching film . . . ether mask, ether vertigo
. . . triangles, spheres, rectangles, pyramids, prisms, coils
go away and come in in regular sequence . . . a coil coming in, two coils coming in, three coils coming in . . . a
coil going away, two coils going away, four going away

A coil straight ahead going away, two coils on the left
and right going away, three coils left right and center going away, four coils right left center and behind going
away

A coil coming, two coils coming in, three coils coming
in, four coils coming in . . . spirals of light . . . round
and round faster faster, baby eaten by rats, hangings, elec-
trocutions, castrations . . .

The RM can be cut in with the most ordinary scenes
covering the planet in a smog of fear . . .

The RM is a built-in electronic police force armed with
hideous threats. You don't want to be a cute little wolf
club? All right, cattle to the slaughter house meat on a
hook.

Here is a nostalgic reconstruction of the old fashioned
Mayan methods. The wrong kind of workers with wrong
thoughts are tortured to death in rooms under the pyra-
mid . . . A young worker has been given a powerful hallucinogen and sexual stimulant . . . Naked he is strapped
down and skinned alive . . . The dark Gods of pain are
surfacing from the immemorial filth of time . . . The
Oaub Bird stands there, screams, watching through his
wild blue eyes. Others are crabs from the waist up clicking
their claws in ecstasy, they dance around and mimic the
flayed man. The scribes are busy with sketches . . . Now
he is strapped into a segmented copper centipede and
placed gently on a bed of hot coals . . . Soon the priests
will dig the soft meat from the shell with their golden
claws . . . Here is another youth staked out on an ant
hill honey smeared on his eyes and genitals . . . Others
with heavy weights on their backs are slowly dragged
through wooden troughs in which shards of obsidian have

been driven . . . So the priests are the masters of pain
and fear and death . . . To do right . . . To obey the
priests . . . To do wrong? The priest's very presence and
a few banal words . . .

The priests postulated and set up a hermetic universe
of which they were the axiomatic controllers. In so doing they became Gods who controlled the known universe
of the workers. They became Fear and Pain, Death and
Time. By making opposition seemingly impossible they
failed to make any provision for opposition. There is
evidence that this control system broke down in some
areas before the arrival of the White God. Stellae have
been found defaced and overturned, mute evidence of a
worker's revolution. How did this happen? The history
of revolutionary movements show that they are usually
led by defectors from the ruling class. The Spanish rule
in South America was overthrown by Spanish revolu-
tionaries. The French were driven out of Algeria by Al-
gerians educated in France. Perhaps one of the priest
Gods defected and organized a worker's revolution . . .

The priest gods in the temple. They move very slowly,
faces ravaged with age and disease. Parasitic worms infest
their dead fibrous flesh. They are making calculations
from the sacred books.

"400,000,000 years ago on this day a grievous thing
happened . . ."

Limestone skulls rain in through the porticos. The
Young Maize God leads the workers as they storm the
temple and drag the priests out. They build a huge brush
fire, throw the priests in and then throw the sacred books
in after them. Time buckles and bends. The old Gods,
surfacing from the immemorial depths of time, burst in
the sky . . . Mr. Hart stands there looking at the broken
stellae . . . "How did this happen?"

His control system must be absolute and world wide.
Because such a control system is even more vulnerable
to attack from without than revolt from within . . . Here
is Bishop Landa burning the sacred books. To give you
an idea as to what is happening, imagine our civilization
invaded by louts from outer space . . .

"Get some bulldozers in here. Clear out all this crap
. . ." The formulae of all the natural sciences, books,
paintings, the lot, swept into a vast pile and burned. And
that's it. No one ever heard of it . . .

Three codices survived the vandalism of Bishop Landa
and these are burned around the edges. No way to know
if we have here the sonnets of Shakespeare, the Mona
Lisa or the remnants of a Sears Roebuck catalogue after
the old out-house burned down in a brush fire. A whole
civilization went up in smoke . . .

When the Spaniards arrived, they found the Mayan
aristocrats lolling in hammocks. Well, time to show them
what is what. Five captured workers bound and stripped,
are castrated on a tree stump, the bleeding, sobbing,
screaming bodies thrown into a pile . . .

"And now get this through your gook nuts. We want
to see a pile of gold that big and we want to see it
pronto. The White God has spoken."

Consider now the human voice as a weapon. To what
extent can the unaided human voice duplicate effects that
can be done with a tape recorder? Learning to speak with
the mouth shut, thus displacing your speech, is fairly
easy. You can also learn to speak backwards, which is
fairly difficult. I have seen people who can repeat what
you are saying after you and finish at the same time. This
is a most disconcerting trick, particularly when practiced
on a mass scale at a political rally. Is it possible to actually
scramble speech? A far-reaching biologic weapon can be
forged from a new language. In fact such a language
already exists. It exists as Chinese, a total language closer
to the multi-level structure of experience, with a script
derived from hieroglyphs, more closely related to the objects and areas described. The equanimity of the Chinese
is undoubtedly derived from their language being struc-
tured for greater sanity. I notice the Chinese, wherever
they are, retain the written and spoken language, while
other immigrant peoples will lose their language in two
generations. The aim of this project is to build a language
in which certain falsifications inherent in all existing
Western languages will be made incapable of formulation.

The follow-falsifications to be deleted from the proposed language.

The IS of Identity. You are an animal. You are a body. Now whatever you may be you are not an "animal," you are not a "body," because these are verbal labels. The IS of identity always carries the implication of that and nothing else, and it also carries the assignment of permanent condition. To stay that way. All naming calling presupposes the IS of identity. This concept is unnecessary in a hieroglyphic language like ancient Egyptian and in fact frequently omitted. No need to say the sun IS in the sky, sun in sky suffices. The verb *to be* can easily be omitted from any language and the followers of Count Korgybski have done this, eliminating the verb *to be* in English. However, it is difficult to tidy up the English language by arbitrary exclusion of concepts which remain in force so long as the unchanged language is spoken.

The definite article THE. THE contains the implication of one and only: THE God, THE universe, THE way, THE right, THE wrong. If there is another, then THAT universe, THAT way is no longer THE universe, THE way. The definite article THE will be deleted and the indefinite article A will take its place.

The whole concept of EITHER/OR. Right or wrong, physical or mental, true or false, the whole concept of OR will be deleted from the language and replaced by juxtaposition, by *and.* This is done to some extent in any pictorial language where the two concepts stand literally side by side. These falsifications inherent in English and other Western alphabetical languages give the reactive mind commands their overwhelming force in the languages. Consider the IS of identity. When I say to be me, to be you, to be myself, to be others—whatever I may be called upon to be or say that I am—I am not the verbal label "myself." I cannot be and am not the verbal label "myself." The word BE in English contains, as a virus contains, its precoded message of damage, the categorical imperative of permanent condition. To be a body, to be nothing else, to stay a body. To be an animal, to be nothing else, to stay an animal. If you see the relation of the I to the body, as the relation of a pilot to his ship, you see the full crippling force of the reactive mind command to be a body. Telling the pilot to be the plane, then who will pilot the plane?

The IS of identity, assigning a rigid and permanent status, was greatly reinforced by the customs and passport control that came in after World War I. Whatever you may be, you are not the verbal labels in your passport any more than you are the word "self." So you must be prepared to prove at all times that you are what you are not. Much of the force of the reactive mind also depends on the falsification inherent in the categorical definite article THE. THE now, THE past, THE time, THE space, THE energy, THE matter, THE universe. Definite article THE contains the implication of no other. THE universe locks you in THE, and denies the possibility of any other. If other universes are possible, then the universe is no longer THE it becomes A. The definite article THE in the proposed language is deleted and replaced by A. Many of the RM commands are in point of fact contradictory commands and a contradictory command gains its force from the Aristotelian concept of either/or. To do everything, to do nothing, to have everything, to have nothing, to do it all, to do not any, to stay up, to stay down, to stay in, to stay out, to stay present, to stay absent. These are in point of fact either/or propositions. To do nothing or everything, to have it all or not any, to stay present or to stay absent. Either/or is more difficult to formulate in a written language where both alternatives are pictorially represented and can be deleted entirely from the spoken language. The whole reactive mind can be in fact reduced to three little words—to be "THE." That is to be what you are not, verbal formulations.

I have frequently spoken of word and image as viruses or as acting as viruses, and this is not an allegorical comparison. It will be seen that the falsifications in syllabic Western languages are in point of fact actual virus mechanisms. The IS of identity is in point of fact the virus mechanism. If we can infer purpose from behavior, then the purpose of a virus is TO SURVIVE. To survive at any expense to the host invaded. To be an animal, to be a body. To be an animal body that the virus can invade. To be animals, to be bodies. To be more animal bodies so that the virus can move from one body to another. To stay present as an animal body, to stay absent as antibody or resistance to the body invasion.

The categorical THE is also a virus mechanism, locking you in THE virus universe. EITHER/OR is another virus formula. It is always you OR the virus. EITHER/OR. This is in point of fact the conflict formula which is seen to be an archetypical virus mechanism. The proposed language will delete these virus mechanisms and make them impossible of formulation in the language. The language will be a tonal language like Chinese, it will also have a hieroglyphic script as pictorial as possible without being too cumbersome or difficult to write. This language will give one the option of silence. When not talking, the user of this language can take in the silent images of the written, pictorial and symbol languages.

I have described here a number of weapons and tactics in the war game. Weapons that change consciousness could call the war game in question. All games are hostile. Basically there is only one game and that game is war. It's the old army game from here to eternity. Mr. Hubbard says that Scientology is a game where everybody wins. There are no games where everybody wins. That's what games are all about, winning and losing . . . The Versailles Treaty . . . Hitler dances the Occupation Jig . . . War criminals hang at Nuremberg . . . It is a rule of this game that there can be no final victory since this would mean the end of the war game. Yet every player must believe in final victory and strive for it with all his power. Faced by the nightmare of final defeat he has no alternative. So all existing technologies with escalating efficiency produce more and more total weapons until we have the atom bomb which could end the game by destroying all players. Now mock up a miracle. The so stupid players decide to save the game. They sit down around a big table and draw up a plan for the immediate deactivation and eventual destruction of all atomic weapons. Why stop there? Conventional bombs are unnecessarily destructive if nobody else has them hein? Let's turn the war clock back to 1917:

> Keep the home fires burning
> Though the hearts are yearning
> There's a long, long trail awinding . . .
> Back to the American Civil War . . .

"He has loosed the fatal lighting of his terrible swift sword." His fatal lightning didn't cost as much in those days. Save a lot on the defense budget this way on back to flintlocks, matchlocks, swords, armor, lances, bows and arrows, spears, stone axes and clubs. Why stop there? Why not grow teeth and claws, poison fangs, stingers, spines, quills, beaks and suckers and stink glands and fight it out in the muck hein?

That is what this revolution is about. End of game. New games? There are no new games from here to eternity. END OF THE WAR GAME.

SCRIBE STREET

Basic Academy Bulletins formulated in 1899:

"Co-education is no education. There are no co-educational academies."

"Students should never be woken up by loud discordant sounds. Music may be used if not too loud or one student is delegated to waken the other students in his section."

"A student who undertakes a wide diversity of unrelated subjects simultaneously will not acquire a useful knowledge of any subject. One subject at a time should be studied until it is thoroughly understood and mastered through both theory and practice. No subject can be learned until the student has the necessary tools and knows how to use them. The first tool the student must learn to use is his own body. In the beginning course emphasis is upon physical drills since control of the body leads to control of the mind."

"All students learn a simplified hieroglyphic script and training in this script is begun immediately after enrollment. The students learn to read and write in this script and to speak in a transliteration from it. The purpose is to decondition the student from automatic verbal reactions by teaching him to think in pictures. The student learns to look before he talks. When he learns to use words instead of being used by them the mastery of any subject becomes easy."

Excerpts from a student's diary: September 17, 1969 ... "I was awakened at 6:30 by train whistles. There are a number of sound effects used for this purpose. We got up washed dressed and reported to the gymnasium where we spend half an hour in karate exercises. The instructor insists that each exercise be perfectly learned before going on to another and since some of us learn faster than others the karate class is divided into several sections. After breakfast and a half-hour reading period we reported for study. There are six students in a study group. The instructor handed us each a copy of the following bulletin:

"Bulletin 'Scribe Street': You are about to learn a simplified script derived from the Egyptian hieroglyphic system. The purpose is to accustom you to thinking in pictures without words and then transliterate back into arbitrary word formulations. Vowel sounds are arbitrarily inserted to form pronounceable words and this constitutes the spoken language which you will also learn. In 1959 Mr Brion Gysin said 'I have found the way to rub out words.' This way was the substitution of arbitrary symbols on the typewriter—(%£&":...7)—for the words of a sentence and a subsequent permutation of these symbols.

"Carrying Mr Gysin's postulate further we must consider the questions of grammar and structure. For example take the following sentence. 'You—(plural)—tell your names to this scribe.' Considered as an English sentence a number of permutations are possible that still make perfect sense::::: 'Tell your names to this scribe, you.' 'You tell this scribe your names too.' 'You tell this scribe your two names.' 'This scribe to tell you your names.' 'Your scribe to tell you your names' etc. Now consider this sentence written in simplified Egyptian hieroglyphs:

Tell	you	name	of you	to	scribe	this

"A picture-language sentence is a statement of events in a certain order in time. The word order is fixed since a picture language depends on juxtaposition for sense and on a juxtaposition that does not change. Permutating this sentence you do not get new or altered meanings. You get no meaning or sense whatever. The pronoun *you* is a suffix pronoun here and can never come before the verb. The object *name* follows the pronoun and is followed by the genetive suffix pronouns *your*—(literally *of you*)—. The proposition *to* can never mean two or in addition to. The demonstrative *this* as used here must always follow its noun. If you should permutate the sentence and then show it to a person who reads hieroglyphs he would simply conclude that he was reading a list of unrelated words. The word order is the meaning. Now suppose one developed a picture writing designed to produce the events written—(the so-called 'Board Books'). It is obvious that the same considerations would apply and any alteration of symbol order would destroy the intention: the events would not happen or would happen differently.

Went he to corner that 4 P.M.
   =   &   =   +   : 16 P.M.

206 · *The job*

"Any alteration of symbol order will alter the sense that is will not put him on a certain corner at 4 P.M. He went gives him a choice. To must have the meaning of direction. That corner might land him some place before the corner. 4 P.M. must end the sentence to indicate his arrival there at that time.

"The Egyptian and Mayan control systems were predicated on the fact that only the ruling caste could read the written language. The supposition now arises that the present control system which we intend to overthrow is predicated on precisely the same consideration: only the self-written elite have access to the 'Board Books.' Control phrases which they place in magazines, newspapers, and in popular songs precisely correspond to a secret picture language. For this reason certain word order in these control phrases is essential. The intention of the control machine is of course to keep word and referent as far separated as possible in order to divert attention from the inferential 'Board Books.'

"It is noteworthy that the grammar of virus has the same unalterable order. Here is the cycle of action of an influenza virus: exposure—(ACHOO)—::: susceptible host:::attachment of the virus to a cell wall:::attachment to other cells:::replication within the cell:::replication within other cells:::release from other cells:::release from the host to invade another susceptible host. Any alteration or permutation of this order and the intention is lost: infection does not occur or is arrested. Mr L. Ron Hubbard has given us an excellent definition of communication: cause, distance, effect, with intention, attention and duplication. More fully stated: 'Communication is the consideration and action of impelling an impulse or particle from source point across a distance to a receipt point with the intention of bringing into being at the receipt point a duplication of that which emanated from the source point.' Applying this definition it will be seen that the virus has achieved a precision of communication with particular reference a duplication of that which emanated from the source point far in advance of human speech. This precision depends on a rigid an unvarying order of programming at the cellular level. You will study in detail the language of the virus in a later course.

"*To destroy in your nervous system the effect of a verbal formulation, and all aberration is based on verbal formulations, you have only to put the words in hieroglyphs and then permutate the order of the symbols.* However, this operation will not work until you have thoroughly familiarized yourself with a picture language. Now look again at the sentence

Tell	you	name	of you	to	scribe	this

"Read it over several times until you identify the symbols with the words. Cover the English translation. You will notice that you can now read without subvocal speech. You will notice further that while the order of symbols is as in English from left to right you do not have to read it symbol by symbol from left to right. In fact you can see and read the sentence as a whole seeing the beginning and end of the sentence at the same time. Once you have learned a picture language you can read much more rapidly. You can in fact absorb a whole page in a matter of seconds...

"We were instructed to read this bulletin over a number of times until we were sure we knew what it meant and to look up in the dictionary any words we did not understand. The instructor gave each of us a copy of the alphabet.

"'Carry this around with you and study it in spare moments. In memorizing material thirty one-minute exposures are more effective than thirty minutes of consecu-

tive study. Memory is not a matter of effort. The first
glyphs you will learn are the commands for the drills you
will be doing this afternoon:

" 'Stand up. Walk over to that chair. Sit down. Take
off your shoes. Take off your socks. Stand up. Take off
your shirt. Put it on back of the chair. Take off your
pants. Fold them on chair. Take off your shorts. Place
them on pants. Put on your shorts. Put on your shirt.
Put on your pants. Sit down. Put on your socks. Put on
your shoes. Stand up. Walk over to that chair. Sit down.'

"The instructor wrote out these sentences in glyphs
and transliteration on the blackboard, and left them there
for thirty seconds. Then we were each requested to write
the sentence in glyphs and transliteration. He ran through
the sentences again and again. This drill lasted four hours
with a fifteen-minute break. At the end of the study
period we were each issued shirt, pants, shoes, socks,
underwear shorts each article marked with the glyphs for
that article: shirt of me, pants of me etc. We were instructed to report back dressed in these clothes following the after-lunch reading period. Reporting back to the
study room we were given another bulletin:

"Bulletin 'Put on a clean shirt and walked out.'::: You
are now going to learn how to dress and undress. You
may think you already know this. Chances are you don't.
You may have heard of the man mentioned in Lord
Chesterfield's letters who killed himself because he could
not stand to dress and undress himself wash and shave.
It wasn't the monotony of these operations that killed
him. It was the fact that he was not performing them
properly. Any action not properly performed becomes increasingly painful. He was not performing these simple
actions properly because he was *not there.* He considered
these actions unimportant so he was thinking about something else while performing them. If you are thinking
about something else while you do something you won't
do it right. That is why you fumble with your shoes and

socks. That is why you leave your shirt half-buttoned to look for your tie or cuff links. That is why you wander out into the hall with one shoe on to see if there is any mail. In dressing as in any other operation *always complete a cycle of action*. When you start to button your shirt finish buttoning your shirt.

"You have just been learning karate exercises and performing movements to which you are not accustomed. As you have noticed this is very painful at first. Soon you will be able to do these exercises with no effort and a good deal of enjoyment. When you learn a new skill you realize the necessity of concentration on what you are doing. However, the actions like dressing that you perform every day, precisely because they seem to have no importance and you think you know how to do them, are in many cases sloppily performed all the days of your life and consequently become increasingly painful and monotonous. So people who can perform quite difficult feats of coordination lose balance while putting on their pants, cut themselves while shaving, crush their hats getting out of a taxi. So present time becomes unendurable. However, an action properly performed with no wasted movements using exactly the amount of effort needed and no more is never a source of pain. Place a number of objects of different weight on a table. Pick up each in turn. Notice that you need to exert more effort to pick up the heavier objects. Exert exactly the degree of effort necessary to pick up each object. Your pants are heavier than your shirt. Do not use the strength required to pick up your pants to pick up your shirt. When you do so you are using arbitrary strength without consideration for the actual object. Do not pick up your pants with shirt strength. They will slip from your fingers.

"You have already completed a course at the Academy of Scientology. You will recognize these exercises as extensions from exercises you have already learned designed to bring you into contact with the objects of your environment to teach you to control these objects and to control the movements and intentions of your own body.

"After we had read the bulletin and the instructor had made sure that we understood it we were instructed to line up six chairs against one wall and six chairs each student facing an empty chair. The instructor gave the orders in transliteration from the glyphs while at the same time each command appeared on a television screen.

" 'Student 1, stand up. Walk over to that chair. Sit down in that chair. Take off your shoes. Take off your socks. Stand up. Take off your shirt. Put your shirt over the chair. Take off your pants. Put on your shorts. Put on your shirt. Put on your pants. Sit down. Put on your socks. Put on your shoes. Stand up. Walk over to that chair. Sit down. Student 2,' and so on down the line.

"Commands and suggestions that we had not learned in glyphs and transliteration were given in English: 'Don't try for speed. Try for precision. No wasted movements. No fumbling. Complete each cycle of action. Contact each garment. Make it your own. Identify it with its symbol. Make it do what you want it to do.'

"After we had undressed and dressed a number of times on the instructor's commands we were told to repeat the cycle immediately without waiting for commands so were all in continuous movement. We spent a week on the undressing and dressing exercises adding more garments, jackets, ties, hats, scarves, overcoats, sweaters, always learning the glyph for each article and operation to be performed in glyphs and transliteration. After the first week clothes seemed to slip onto my body of themselves. I could dress and undress with unbelievable smoothness and speed. The exercises were extended. We folded clothes and put them away in drawers and shelves. We emptied laundry bags, made out laundry lists, put the clothes back emptied the bag again and made out new lists. We made and unmade beds. We packed and unpacked suitcases. We performed various serial actions involving keys, passports, watches, brief cases, tickets, suitcases. As the actions performed became more complex we wrote out in glyphs and transliteration the precise order of the actions to be performed. We set up dummy restaurants in which the students were the waiters, patrons and cashiers. We learned to handle money and make change. As training stress the student cashiers and waiters always tried to overcharge or shortchange. 'Never allow yourself to be overcharged, cheated or shortchanged. Overall defeat in life is made up of many small defeats.'

"After two months we are able to think entirely in glyphs and to converse in transliterations. The words I now use refer to actual objects and operations I have controlled and made my own. We are now ready for the more advanced exercises. We will learn to write out the actions of a whole day in glyphs and to carry out those actions precisely. We will learn to confuse opponents by carrying on a banal 'friendly' conversation while thinking in hostile insulting glyphs and communicating those pictures to the opponents."

HOW TO BE HUMPHREY BOGART

The scene is a projection-room stage in front of a screen audience of twelve men cool and impassive in deep leather chairs.

B.J. is seated to the right of the stage at a control panel. He can see both the stage and the audience.

"It's the hottest thing in show biz since the Old Man pulled Eve out of Adam and right under our nose since the first magic lantern."

A young man brings a chair on to the stage and sits down in front of the screen facing the audience. A tinted photo of Jesse James is projected onto his face and focused to fit exactly.

"See what I mean? A picture projected on flesh is flesh. Now lets give J.J. some background."

On screen reconstructed 1882 room Missouri farm-
house Death of Stonewall Jackson on the wall. The picture is dusty.

"What you have just seen is done with two magic
lanterns one projected on the actor's face and the other
on backdrop...still pictures show the simplest applica-
tion."

Stonewall Jackson, Daniel Boone and Daniel Webster
follow Jesse James on the stage.

"Talk about modeling yourself on the great Americans
... Now for color film talking."

Another young man brings a chair on to the stage
and sits down in front of the screen. They are the same
height and build dressed in identical white suits. One is
blond the other dark.

"I'm Joe" says the blond.

"I'm John" says the dark boy.

A color picture of John is projected on to Joe. The
face says "I'm John."

A color picture of Joe is projected on to John. The
face says "I'm Joe."

"What you are seeing and hearing now is film and
pre-recorded sound track. The actors are silent in this
sequence."

Now slowly Joe and John change seats.

"Notice how the projector just picks them up and carries them from one seat to the other. Even with the
stills you can feel it take hold and mold your face. If the
projector moves slowly to the left it will turn your head
to the left. All right shift."

They change seats faster this time.

"I'm Joe"

"I'm John"

"faster faster round and round"

"I'm Joe I'm John"

"faster faster"

"ImJoeImJohn"

They stand now at the front of the stage and bow in their projected faces.

"Anybody know which is Joe and which is John? Another face on your face talking gives you the feeling you are that person. Now let's see what Joe and John can do without the projectors."

They sit side by side.

Joe says "I'm John" in John's voice.

John in Joe's voice says "I'm Joe."

"Notice how you can see Joe in John's face and John in Joe's face. Take it away boys."

Joe stands up in full-length projection of a pop singer and sings a rock-and-roll number.

John joins him in another pop singer and they do a duet tossing faces lyrics and hips back and forth.

"Gives you a funny feeling doesn't it?"

One man takes a cigar out of his mouth the ash held in a delicate grey cone the way it holds on a really expensive cigar. "Maybe a little too funny B.J."

"Round and round the projector goes where it stops nobody knows."

The projectors shut off.

"Now see how they do without projectors."

The boys sing almost perfect imitations of the pop stars.

"You see the angle? We put out projection units with synchronized sound track. You can be your favorite pop star. You can be your favorite actor living or dead."

Joe and John sitting at café table backdrop shows Arab market. John is a seedy lapsed Catholic from a Graham Greene novel on a dangerous mission he doesn't really believe in. Joe is a young American seaman with pale grey eyes. We don't know what is going to happen. Neither do Joe and John. They find out as the action unfolds.

"A field test at the experimental stage..."

The older man looks across the square: one frame flash

of burning cars blackened bodies "I mean if the test were only partially successful..." He fingers a cyanide ring absently. The seaman seems to be looking at some distant point far away and long ago.

"Success is always partial."

"You don't just look at the action you take part in it. Of course this will revolutionize the blue movies. Strip down and dive in..."

Warning from the Board of Health: "The projection of sex films on flesh can give rise to venereal diseases hitherto unknown. It is strongly urged that such experiments as full-length nude projection be shelved pending more precise data from less dangerous experiments."

Projection units proved an ideal method for learning languages. Any teacher you want plenty of pictures to pick from fill in some background with the other projector and there you are Latin Quarter café chattering away in French for he knew the language. Just sit back and listen to your teaching skin talk. You will soon understand what your skin is saying and you will soon be able to say it. There is a moment when you feel it take. In fact projections proved an accelerated method of acquiring any skill: public speaking, salesmanship, swindling, seduction, hypnotism, acting, yoga, perfect poise. Any verbal or facial adaptation you fancy just buy the suitable projection kit. You want to look younger? Buy a Youth Kit. You want to look dignified? Buy a Dignity Kit. You want to look happy? Buy a Smile Kit. You want to look seductive? Buy a Seduction Kit. You want to look confusing? Buy a Scramble Kit that alternates expressions 24 frames per second. You want to look saintly? Buy a Saint Kit. You want to look inscrutable? Buy an Inscrutable Kit. You want to look brave? Buy a Courage Kit. You want to embarrass your enemy? Buy an Ugly-Awkward Kit and flash it on him. You want to louse up a speaker? Buy a Stutter-Stumble-Tongue-Tie-Voice-Break-Stupid-Fidget-Twitch Kit. You want to make your enemy sick? There's a kit for every disease in the book. You want to kill your enemy? Buy a Death Kit. Every variety of projector gun from 8 mm hand guns for point-blank range to lasers with Questar telescopic sights came into use. Secret agents had their cover projected on them till it grew there. Anybody who wanted to change his life could take his pick of New Identity Kits.

Projector pop groups sprang up everywhere drawing their fans into the act swelled to hundreds then thousands with transport trucks and camp kitchen defying all immigration and customs control. No one wanted to argue with the wandering singers. To list but a few: The Spastic Swans left a wake of trays and glasses flying into the air uncontrolled knees, elbows and feet kicking out store front crashing through windows.

The Buful Peoples came out with a horrible number called "Here Me Is." Seems the infant son of Buful Bradly would hide himself behind a sofa or under a desk and pop out saying "Here me is" and that gave him the idea. The stage is an empty room and then the Buful Peoples start popping out in baby faces saying "Here Me Is" and shooting the audience with projection guns. Thousands of fans went mad, put on diapers and rushed through the streets shitting and pissing themselves as they screamed out:

"HERE ME IS" "HERE ME IS" "HERE ME IS."

The Board of Health issued a powerfully worded warning relative to "the danger to health mental moral and physical posed by the hideous practice of baby-talking or still worse baby-singing adults."

The Rolling Bones killed ten thousand fans in their seats with a rousing rendition of "Good Little Bad Little You" alternating sweet and vicious 24 times per second.

The projections were posed by professional actors at first but there is nothing like the real thing: real happy faces, pain faces, death faces. Souped up studio trucks prowl the streets ready to jump out on anybody. The

young terrorist shot by a firing squad in Vietnam is
hardly cold before a million mad queens are soaking up
his death. They go around looking younger for a few
days then they need MORE MORE MORE. It was all
rather like the Aztecs once people got a smell of blood
there was no holding them and soon they are quite frankly
killing people for the pictures and gut whole communities like a plague of locusts. The Soviet Representative
rose in the UN today to denounce what he termed "vile
bloodsucking vampires leeching youth of the world
through film projectors."

The old millionaire has a film studio at his deathbed
to take his last words and the heirs have to sit still for the
old man's death pictures each anniversary so they won't
be forgetting where the money came from. Company
presidents project themselves on all their employees.
Political figures populate whole countries with their
projected image. And you never know when some wise
guy is projecting on you from the other side of town
through his Questar. It amounts to an all-out image
contest and there can be only one end to that. The end
is one face: Mr Who??

The first use in show business of projections as here
described was a performance put on by Brion Gysin and
Ian Sommerville at The American Centre, rue Dragon,
Paris, France in January of 1962. The audience could not
believe what they saw. They thought the whole sequence
was pre-photographed. In this performance slide projectors were used.

To get results use only color pictures. It is most important that the projection be fitted precisely onto a face.
This is easy with stills. Moving pictures require more
precision in preparing the sequence to be projected.

Q : You have said that the "academy series" offers a solution to the problem of alienated youth and to many
other problems as well. Would you enlarge on that point?

A : The first academies were established in September of
1899 one on a mesa north of Santa Fe New Mexico, one
outside St Louis, Missouri, and one on the Hudson outside New York City. Since Eastern systems like yoga,
judo, karate, aikido, zen were part of the training instructors were invited from the Orient and Eastern students
came to learn Western techniques. The basic aim of the
academies was to synthesize the most functional aspects
of Eastern and Western training. Academy graduates, returning to various professions, proved themselves incom-
parably more efficient than those who had not received
academy training so more and more academies were set
up. Other countries followed America's lead in setting up
academies the continual interchange of students and instructors tending to break down national boundaries. By
the end of the 1920's there were academies throughout
the world directing all research, education, police action
and political formulations. The academies were located
in sites of great beauty the architecture suited to the land
scape. The Marrakesh academy was built around a vast
courtyard with gardens and trees pools fountains and
porticos. There were a number of academies in the Amazon rain forest intricate structures of heavy timbers and
split bamboo connected by catwalks and ladders. Here the
physical training was carried out through canoe trips hunt-
ing fishing and farming the program of training being
adapted to the country and the landscape. The Eastern
academies often used existing temples and monasteries
and one of the most spectacular academies was built into
the restored ruins of Samarkand. For the Greek academy
all Greek antiquities scattered through museums of the
world were assembled. Dead fragments of Sunday curiosity were molded everywhere into living structures. The
canal city of Mexico was reconstructed and Mayan ruins
echoed to the ancient language which all students at this
academy were requested to master—(Mayan is very much
a living language and in the remote villages of Yucatan

nothing else is spoken). Always the emphasis was on interchange of cultures languages and training methods.

The St Louis academy was a rambling red brick building on a bluff over the river. A twilight-like blue dust was
settling into the river valley when Bill Harper a beginning
student descended from a horse-drawn carriage cool remote Sunday fresh southerly winds a long time ago room
with rose wallpaper copper luster washbasins an Indian
boy got up off one of the brass beds and introduced himself

"I am Johnny Bufeo from the Ucyalli. I will go on to
the medical school as I am son of a *brujo.* He had many
remedies and only some of them were good. He could
bring rain and he could call animals and sometimes he
could kill a sick enemy. I have seen him draw fear from
a patient with his dirty old hands and so many times I
had to tell the patients 'very sorry the *brujo* is slobbed
out borracho.' He dies many years ago. American doctors
could learn from him. I am here to teach and to learn.
You get plenty strong plenty tough here. Then you go
into silence rooms learn leave body go any place what you
want. You come with me Meester William?"

Roommates were shifted every month rotation being
a basic principle of the academies. Many Western students elected to attend the Eastern academies where they
learned the language and the local disciplines. Some students shifted from one academy to the other every three
months and instructors also rotated from Marrakesh to
the fjords of Norway from Missouri to Samarkand. Instructors and advanced students in the specialized academies would return to the basic academy course to refresh
themselves with physical training and impart their knowledge to beginning students by direct contact. All academies exchanged weekly bulletins on research, experiments,
and new methods of training. With the advent of tape
recorders and movie cameras films and tapes were constantly exchanged. Students with camera and recorder

wandered from one academy to the other and guest rooms were set aside for the wandering students. While the training varied from one academy to the other there were certain courses of training common to all: karate, judo, aikido, zen, breathing exercises to achieve perfect health and control of the body, silence drills in sense-withdrawal chambers and immersion tanks, and the mastery of a simplified hieroglyphic script teaching the students to think in silent images. The basic academy course lasted four years. After graduation from the basic academy students could apply for advanced training at one of the specialized academies. In the medical school the students learned in addition to the standard Western techniques all forms of massage, osteopathy, remedial exercises and diet. They studied the techniques of witch doctors and faith healers and examined samples of all herbal and jungle remedies to isolate the active principles and apply them to therapy.

At the time the first academies were founded heroin, cocaine and morphine were sold across the counter in drug stores. A survey revealed that there were 200,000 addicts in the United States many of whom had become addicted through the use of patented preparations. The addicts were for the most part middle aged or elderly suffering from various chronic illnesses. On recommendation of the academies opiates with the exception of codeine were distributed only on prescription. Once novocaine was synthesized the extraction of cocaine was discontinued and this drug disappeared from the pharmacopœia. Confirmed addicts were allowed a maintenance dose of opium or morphine whereas the use of heroin was restricted to medical use in the relief of extreme pain. A program of study was undertaken to determine the most efficacious treatment for addiction with particular reference to young addicts. The apomorphine treatment was used and during the 1930's the formula was synthesized and a number of variations were developed. The regulatory action of apomorphine led to the concept of preventative medicine with the emphasis on maintaining health rather than curing sickness.

"Anything that can be done chemically can be done in other ways...what is missed in withdrawal is a certain frequency." Academy Bulletin June 19, 1922

The frequency of opiates turned out to be a special oscillation of ultra sound. The frequency was quite as habit-forming as morphine but could be gradually shut off over a period of several months resulting in a painless cure. Since it was a rule in the academies that all beginning students must refrain from the use of any drug including alcohol and tobacco and all young people aspired to graduate from the academies they were easily conditioned to avoid addicting drugs once cure was accomplished. The discovery that the effects of morphine can be produced by a sound frequency led to realization that the effects of any drug can be so produced and frequency therapy came to supplant drug therapy. The training of all police was carried out by the academies, and only graduates of the police academies could qualify as police officers. The cadet officers were taught to prevent crime and keep people out of jail. Stop that swindler in Toronto before he issues any worthless mining stock. That man with a killer's temper should not be running a bar. Parents who don't want their children should have the children taken away from them before abuse occurs. All cases of cruelty to children received special attention and every patrolman was expected to know about infractions in his district. The protection of children was an interim measure pending the slow abolition of the old family system after which the rearing of children from birth would be in the hands of special centers set up by the academies. Such centers were already in existence to take care of abandoned or unwanted children.

The sign of a well-run country is few police and few laws but those laws really enforced and those police

221 • *Academy 23*

really efficient. The whole system of state legislators was abolished and a uniform code of laws drawn up covering crimes against person and crimes against property. All so-called offenses involving private sexual behavior, drugs and gambling were eliminated from the legal code.

A.S.—Academy Security—was the highest police agency concerning itself with any unhealthy influences impeding the work of the academies. A.S. was not able to stop the first World War but did manage to keep America out of it. After the war they were in position to avoid the debacle of prohibition and the concomitant infiltration of the Mafia

"A pestiferous organization that must be dissolved at its very roots"

A.S. moved to curtail the influence of the daily press by eliminating all coverage of crime and accidents

"The daily press is largely responsible for the dreary events they describe... We recommend that all daily papers be discontinued"

The discoveries made by the academies were reported in weekly bulletins so that a discovery made anywhere was immediately available throughout the world. There was nothing secret about academy research.

"Admittedly any important discovery can be misused. However, if the destructive potentials of a discovery be kept secret its monopoly and misuse by a self-styled elite poses a more cogent threat than the possibility that some individual might misuse the discovery when it is made common knowledge. For example the destructive potentials of infra sound have been openly described in our bulletins and we feel that this open-bank policy is the best insurance against the misuse of knowledge since anyone using infra sound for unworthy ends would be immediately detected."

World War II was easily averted by mediation efforts of the French German and English academies and in consequence no atomic weapons were developed

"No release of radioactivity can be allowed to occur."
Academy Bulletin August 4, 1945

The Linguistic Institute carried out experiments with sound and human speech to discover what words are. Subvocal speech was investigated with sensitive throat microphones. Special attention was given to schizophrenic subjects since in this condition involuntary movements of the vocal apparatus are most pronounced giving rise to the "voice" typical of this illness. These "voices" were recorded and played back to the patient cut up slowed down inched speeded up. The playback often resulted in a pronounced improvement. The subjects were then given silence drills. At the prospect of silence many of them became hysterical that is the "voices" became hysterical and were more easily recorded

"YOU CAN'T! YOU CAN'T! YOU CAN'T!" they scream.

Injections of curare were given in these cases to paralyze the vocal apparatus while the subject was in an iron lung. Silence often resulted in a complete remission of the illness.

"Compulsive verbal patterns are actually word viruses that maintain themselves in the central nervous system by manipulation of the speech centers, throat muscles and vocal cords."

The peculiar style of schizophrenic speech was analyzed. It was observed that verbalizing which occurs during dreams and particularly between sleep and waking partakes of the same style and is in fact a special language probably operating at all times in so-called normal individuals. The Linguistic Institute set out to isolate this language and learn it. Students kept recorders by their beds since verbalization in this area is usually forgotten if not immediately recorded or written down. This language has no landmarks by which it can be recalled as if a resident of the psyche were speaking in an unknown language not unknown as regards the words themselves but as regards referents construction and syntax.

The Linguistic Institute also carried out advanced courses in silence training. These installations were located in areas of natural silence the Sahara and Gobi deserts, the high mountains of Tibet and South America. Silence is a medium in which the students slowly learn to breathe until they can stay there for hours with no movements of the throat muscles and vocal cords. A silence frequency of infra sound was developed that vibrates the words loose from the body and this device was used in the last stages of training a slow resonance that grows in the neck and spinal column and reaches deep into the internal organs vibrating the whole body shaking the words loose visible as a haze. At this point many students feel as if a parasitic being has been shaken loose from the body to dissolve reluctantly into air. After the baptism of silence the student moves with ease in the soundless medium but words are at his disposition when he needs them to be used with absolute precision.

During the early days of aviation the academies established centers to train pilots and when space travel became possible they took over direction of the space program. The aim of the academy space program was not space in an aqualung trailing wires to wives and mothers.

"To put quite ordinary individuals into space at enormous expense is nothing to the purpose. Any academy graduate could learn more about space conditions and travel further in space after an hour of weightless silence than teams of orbiting astronauts who do not dream in space. Space *is* dream. Space *is* illusion. Why move a PX with all your dreary verbal preconceptions to the moon?"

The astronauts were all single men since they are trained to exist in total independence and total solitude whereas marriage conditions to dependence.

"To travel in space you must learn to leave the old verbal garbage behind: God talk, priest talk, mother talk, family talk, love talk, party talk, country talk. You must learn to exist with no religion no country no allies. You must learn to see what is in front of you with no pre-conceptions."

Now contrast the possibilities opened by such academies with what we see in the world today. Research that could be used to free the human spirit is being monopolized by paltry intellects in the name of "national security." What are you getting out of national security?

One academy could bring back hope to dead radioactive riot-torn streets to this contaminated overpopulated mismanaged planet. Are they going to give you that hope? If past performance is any indication they are not going to give you anything but bullshit, blacks and whites you have been sold out. If you want the world you could have in terms of discoveries and resources now in existence be prepared to fight for that world. To fight for that world in the streets.

William S. Burroughs
October 15, 1968
London